Rebel Without A Cause

Jorge Consuegra

FADE IN.

A deep night sky. Matte shot. Camera searches slowly upward through the heavens and the silver tone of a bell is heard sounding the strokes of midnight.

On the final note of the bell, camera is full on the Milky Way and there it rests, just long enough for a burst of Easter singing to arise. The hymn is sung by the crude, unmatched voices of children. Camera pans down to include:

Spire of a church. Camera continues its downward pan as the singing continues and we pass a window beyond which is the source of the singing. Camera pans off window to show--

Long shot. City. Night. Suddenly revealed--crisp and sparkling with lights. Camera pans down and over:

A lonely street full of parked cars. The singing diminishes but a thread of it remains. A car has just parked. The headlights snap off. A MAN emerges whistling the same melody and pulls some gifts from the front seat. He slams the door and starts down the street in the direction of a house with bright windows. He must pass an empty lot full of rusty grass and litter which lies in darkness between two street lights.

As the MAN walks by the lot, still whistling, a GROUP OF FIGURES rises silently from the grass, figures who have been lying in concealment until now. They step noiselessly onto the pavement and follow the MAN. At the sound of their boots the whistling stops.

The MAN glances behind him and sees the figures walking after him, filling the pavement. A street light shows them to be boys and girls and all quite young. The MAN moves on more swiftly and the sound of their pursuit increases. He begins to run toward the lighted house and the following steps run too. Suddenly he stops under the next street light and turns to face the figures. They are upon him and around him quickly. Nobody speaks for a moment, then one of the boys grins. His name is BUZZ. He is big and filled with an awareness of his own masculinity.

BUZZ
(friendly, cool)
That was pretty what you were whistling. Whistle some more.

The MAN whistles a nervous phrase, trying to make a joke of the situation which he doesn't understand.

BUZZ
(continuing; suddenly)
You got a cigarette?

MAN
Oh, I think so--

The MAN fumbles in his pocket, finds a pack and drops it in his nervousness. The FIGURES wait until he picks it up. He offers one to BUZZ.

MAN
(continuing)
Filter tips.

BUZZ
(smiling, encouraging)
You smoke it. Smoke it, Dad.
Smiling uncertainly, the MAN puts the cigarette in his mouth.
BUZZ, still smiling, takes out a packet of wooden matches.

BUZZ
(continuing)
I'll light it for you, Dad.
BUZZ ignites a match and holds it near the Man's face for a second, searching it. Then he ignites the whole box under his nose. The MAN shrieks, and his packages fall. BUZZ slaps him sharply, his smile gone.
The camera pans away as the figures enclose him, and holds on a small mechanical monkey which has dropped from its wrappings. It begins to dance madly on the pavement, then runs down.
The feet of the figures scatter past the unmoving monkey.
Then camera rises to show that the man has disappeared.
There is a moment of awful stillness, then we see a boy coming down the street alone. He is quite drunk, and he slips once. This is JIM, a good-looking kid of seventeen with a crew-cut and wearing a good suit. The spilled packages on the pavement stop him. He bends down to see what they are and picks up the mechanical monkey from the wreckage. He smiles and winds it up. He sets it on the sidewalk and sits down. He watches it dance for a moment, happily. A siren is heard distantly, growing louder. JIM pays no attention to it as he winds the monkey again and releases it for its dance.
SUPERIMPOSE TITLE: "REBEL WITHOUT A CAUSE" STARRING _____ as siren rises piercingly close, and JIM looks up, we:

DISSOLVE TO:
Close shot. Throbbing light of police car. Night. The siren screaming wildly, then dying. The sound of brakes.
Camera moves to reveal the police car stopped at the entrance of a Precinct Station. Two officers dismount, bearing between them the struggling JIM. They bear him up the steps and in through the double doors.
Inside precinct station. Reception area. A large open space onto which several corridors converge. In the middle is a Sergeant's desk, really a quadrangular counter in the center of which the SERGEANT stands. There are a few glass-walked interviewing rooms which open off the area, and several benches lining the walls. The scene is one of confusion, activity and waiting. Phones ring. The arrested pass in custody of officers. Present among others at JIM's entrance are: JUDY, who is blonde and sixteen. She sits on a crowded bench wearing an expression of downcast bitterness. On a bench across the way from her are three remarkably dirty little Mexican children without shoes or socks. The oldest is a BOY of four who is protecting his little SISTER who in turn mothers an infant crying on the bench beside her.
Standing at a corner of the desk is a docile, undersized boy of fifteen named JOHN "PLATO" CRAWFORD. He is shivering.

With him is a large NEGRO WOMAN, his maid. JIM comes through the doors and is led to the desk. One of the officers presents a brief report to the SERGEANT, who examines it.

SERGEANT
Mixed up in that beating on Twelfth
Street?

OFFICER
No. Plain drunkenness.

SERGEANT
This says he was picked up there.

OFFICER
They had him on the carpet for an hour at Headquarters. He's clear.
Plain drunkenness.

SERGEANT
Young squirt. All right--You want to lean him against something?
Stand him over there.
The officer leads JIM to JUDY's bench and stands him against the wall beside it.
JIM is frisked, a look of prayer on his upturned face. The OFFICER finds the toy monkey in his pocket and would take it, but when JIM asks to keep it, the OFFICER hands it back and moves away. Another officer enters and leads the prisoner who is sitting next to JUDY into another room. JIM sits beside her. He smiles at her but receives only a chilling look. He winds the monkey up and sets it dancing on the floor, but she is not amused. Camera pans to show others reacting to the monkey with pleasure. We see PLATO look up and smile a little. Camera stops on the MEXICAN CHILDREN who are smiling too. A bald JUVENILE OFFICER named
GENE, squats before them, smiling.

GENE
You going to tell me your name now?
The little boy shakes his head.

LITTLE BOY
(touching GENE's bald pate)
Where's your hair?

GENE
It's all gone.

LITTLE BOY
Did you get a haircut?

GENE
No--it just fell out!

LITTLE BOY
(sympathetically)
Aw--
GENE laughs as another Juvenile Officer enters and pauses to look at the children. His
name is RAY.

RAY
What gang does he belong to?

GENE
Give him a couple of years.

RAY
Where's your mamma, honey?

LITTLE BOY
I don't know.
RAY and GENE exchange looks, then RAY moves across to JUDY-- camera following.
He looks down at her, consults the file in his hand.

RAY
Judy--we're ready for you now.

JUDY
(a mumble)
He hates me.

RAY
What?

JUDY
He hates me.
She rises. RAY leads her to one of the glass-walled offices.
Camera moves with them. JIM watches them go.

RAY
What makes you think he hates you,
Judy?

JUDY
I don't think. I know. He looks at me like I'm the ugliest thing in the world. He doesn't
like my friends--he--
RAY leads her into the office.

Inside small office as JUDY comes in, RAY following. He indicates a chair for her while he sits down behind a desk.

JUDY
(continuing)
He doesn't like anything about me-- he calls me--he calls me--
She starts to cry. She doesn't hide it, but keeps wiping the tears with the palms of her hands.

RAY
He makes you feel pretty unhappy?

JUDY
(crying)
He calls me a dirty tramp--my own father!

RAY
Do you think your father means that?

JUDY
Yes! I don't know! I mean maybe he doesn't mean it but he acts like he does. We're altogether and we're going to celebrate Easter and catch a double bill. Big deal. So I put on my new dress and I came out and he--

RAY
That one?

JUDY
Yes--he started yelling for a handkerchief--screaming. He grabbed my face and he rubbed all my lipstick off--he rubbed till I thought I wouldn't have any lips left. And all the time yelling at me--that thing--the thing I told you he called me. Then I ran out of the house.

RAY
Is that why you were wandering around at one o'clock in the morning?

JUDY
I was just talking a walk. I tried to call the kids but everybody was out and I couldn't find them. I hate my life. I just hate it.

RAY
You weren't looking for company, were you?

JUDY
No.

RAY
Did you stop to talk to anyone,
Judy?
(she is silent)
Do you enjoy that?

JUDY
No. I don't even know why I do it.

RAY
Do you think you can get back at your Dad that way? I mean sometimes if we can't get
as close to somebody as we'd like we have to try making them jealous--so they'll have
to pay attention. Did you ever think of that?

JUDY
I'll never get close to anybody.

RAY
Some kids stomped a man on Twelfth
Street, Judy.

JUDY
You know where they picked me up!
Twelfth Street! I wasn't even near there!

RAY
Would you like to go home if we can arrange it?
(no answer; to WOMAN OFFICER)
Did you notify the parents?

WOMAN OFFICER
She wouldn't give me their number.

RAY
What's your number, Judy? We'll see if your Dad will come and get you.
JUDY looks up hopefully.

RAY
Unless you really don't want to go home.
(silence)
Would you rather stay here?
Camera moves close on JUDY. She looks up and speaks very quietly.

JUDY
Lexington 05549.

The wail of a siren is heard. JUDY looks off through the glass wall toward JIM. RAY is heard dialing.
Med. shot. JIM's bench. JIM sits with his head back, eyes closed. As the siren mounts louder, JIM opens his mouth and imitates it--a long, forlorn wail.
Med. shot, PLATO and NEGRO WOMAN. PLATO smiles faintly and moves out toward JIM, NEGRO WOMAN following. Camera pans with them. PLATO sits by JIM. She stands over them. JIM's wailing continues.
Med. shot. JIM, PLATO, NEGRO WOMAN. An OFFICER moves into shot.

OFFICER
Hey!
JIM continues for a moment.

OFFICER
(continuing)
Hey! That's enough static out of you.

JIM
Want me to imitate a stupid cop?

OFFICER
Cut it out now. I'm warning you.

JIM
Yes, ma'am.
The OFFICER moves out. The NEGRO WOMAN bends over PLATO who is shivering violently.

NEGRO WOMAN
You shivering, John? You cold?
PLATO shakes his head. JIM notices him.

JIM
Want my jacket?
PLATO looks up at JIM.

JIM
(continuing)
You want my jacket? It's warm.
PLATO wants it but shakes his head "no."
Full shot. JUDY's office. RAY and JUDY seated as before.
JUDY is still gazing through the glass.

RAY
Your mother will be down in a few minutes, Judy--

JUDY
(clearing)
What?

RAY
Your mother will be down in a few minutes.

JUDY
(startled)
My mother?
RAY signals to a WOMAN OFFICER just outside and leads JUDY to the door.
Outside door as RAY turns JUDY over to the WOMAN OFFICER.

RAY
She's being called for.

JUDY
You said you'd call my father.

RAY
Goodbye, Judy. Take it easy.
JUDY doesn't answer. RAY goes back inside as camera leads the WOMAN OFFICER
and JUDY past JIM's bench. Camera stops on JIM, PLATO and the NEGRO WOMAN.
JIM stares at JUDY and whistles but gets no reaction. GENE enters and comes to the

NEGRO WOMAN.
GENE
John Crawford?

NEGRO WOMAN
Yes, sir.

GENE
Come with me, John.
PLATO rises and goes with GENE, the NEGRO WOMAN following.
JIM is alone. He closes his eyes, throws his head back and gives another siren wail as
camera moves close on his face.

MOTHER (O.S.)
Jim!
JIM looks up suddenly, scared. Then he smiles mysteriously and staggers to his feet.
Low angle. Tight three. JIM's parents and grandma framed in the doorway, frozen. They
are all dressed in evening clothes. The MOTHER is a very chic but rather hard-faced
woman. The FATHER is an unfeathered man. The GRANDMA is the smallest, also
very chic and very bright-eyed.
Med. shot. JIM as he faces them.

JIM
Happy Easter.
Tight shot. The family.

MOTHER
Where were you tonight? They called us at the club and I got the fright of my life!
Silence.

FATHER
Where were you tonight, Jimbo?
Close shot. JIM. He says nothing.
Close shot. FATHER laughing uncomfortably.
Med. shot. JIM.

JIM
You think I'm funny?
JIM turns suddenly and walks to the glass wall of the office behind which PLATO, the
NEGRO WOMAN and GENE are visible.
He looks through the glass partition which separates him from PLATO.

JIM
(continuing)
Why didn't you take my jacket?
Inside office. JIM is seen through the glass. He moves away. PLATO is still shivering,
cracking his knuckles.

GENE
Do you know why you shot those puppies, John?
(silence)
Is that what they call you or do you have a nickname?

PLATO
(a murmur)
Plato.

NEGRO WOMAN
You talk to the man nice now, hear?
He's going to help you.

PLATO
Nobody can help me.

GENE
Can you tell me why you killed the puppies, Plato?

PLATO
No, sir. I just went next door to look at them like I always do.
They were nursing on their mother and I did it. I guess I'm just no good?

GENE
What do you think's going to happen, you do things like that?

PLATO
I don't know. End up in the electric chair?

GENE
Where did you get the gun?

PLATO
In my mother's drawer.

NEGRO WOMAN
She keep it to protect herself, sir.
She scared without a man in the house.

GENE
Where's your mother tonight, Plato?

PLATO
She's away.

NEGRO WOMAN
Seems like she's always going somewhere. She got a sister in
Chicago and she go for the holiday.
She says her sister is all the family she has.

GENE
Where's your father?
PLATO is silent.

NEGRO WOMAN
They not together, sir. We don't see him in a long time now.

GENE
Do you hear from him, son?
PLATO looks up as JIM and his family move into the next office. JIM smiles at PLATO,
who returns it feebly, then looks away embarrassed.

GENE
You know if the boy ever talked to a psychiatrist?

PLATO
(smiling a bit)
Head-shrinker?

NEGRO WOMAN
(laughing)
Oh, Mrs. Crawford don't believe in them!

GENE
Well maybe she better start.
Other office. JIM, his parents, GRANDMA and RAY are gathered in the small room.
JIM is humming THE RIDE OF THE
VALKRYIES to himself as if he had absolutely no interest in what is happening around
him. RAY suspects this is something more than mere disinterest, so lets the humming
go on, in order to discover its real purpose. GRANDMA watches everything like a
tennis match, reacting with soft little sounds of terror or astonishment or sympathy. No
one pays any attention to her. For a moment no one talks. RAY watches JIM as he hums.
Then the FATHER shakes his head and looks up.

FATHER
I don't see what's so bad about taking a little drink.

RAY
You don't?

FATHER
No. I definitely don't. I did the sa--

RAY
He's a minor, Mr. Stark, and it looks to me like he had more than a little drink.

FATHER
(chuckling)
Say, listen--

MOTHER
(to JIM: in intimate, half-humorous disapproval)
Jim--don't hum.
JIM merely rolls his eyes at her, then away--but continues his humming.

FATHER
I guess I cut pretty loose in my day too.

MOTHER
Really, Frank? When was that?

FATHER
Listen--can't you wait till we get home?

RAY
Whoa! Whoa! I know you're a little upset but--

FATHER
Sorry.

RAY
What about you, Jim? Got anything to say for yourself?
JIM stops humming and shrugs.

RAY
Not interested, huh?
JIM shakes his head.

MOTHER
Can't you answer? What's the matter with you anyhow?

FATHER
He's just loaded, honey.

MOTHER
I was talking to Jim.

FATHER
(to RAY)
Let me just explain to you--we just moved here, y'understand? The kid has no friends
yet and--

JIM
Tell him why we moved here.

FATHER
Hold it, Jim.

JIM
You can't protect me.

FATHER
(to JIM)
You mind if I try? You have to slam the door in my face?
(to RAY)
I try to get to him--what happens?
(to JIM)

Don't I give you everything you want? A bicycle--you get a bicycle.
A car--

JIM
You buy me many things. Thank you.

FATHER
Not just buy! You hear all this talk about not lovely your kids enough. We give you
love and affection, don't we?
Silence; JIM is fighting his emotion but his eyes grow wet.

FATHER
Then what is it? I can't even touch you anymore but you pull away.
I want to understand you. Why'd you get drunk? You must have had a reason.
JIM stares straight ahead, trying not to listen.

FATHER
Was it because we went to that party?
(silence)
You know what kind of drunken brawls those parties turn into-- it's no place for kids.

MOTHER
A minute ago you said you didn't care if he drinks.

GRANDMA
He said a little drink.

JIM
(exploding)
You're tearing me apart!

MOTHER
What?

JIM
Stop tearing me apart! You say one thing and he says another and then everybody
changes back--

MOTHER
That's a fine way to behave!

GRANDMA
(smiling)
Well you know who he takes after!

RAY

Outside, Jim. Come outside.
RAY pushes him out the door firmly, and into office vacated by PLATO and GENE.

RAY
Excuse us a minute?

FATHER
(very overwrought)
Sure. Sure.
GENE's office. RAY and JIM alone.

JIM
Someone should put poison in her epsom salts.

RAY
Grandma?
No answer. JIM turns away from RAY.

JIM
Get lost.

RAY
Hang loose, boy. I'm warning you.

JIM
Wash up and go home.

RAY
Big tough character. You don't kid me, pal. How come you're not wearing your boots?
Suddenly JIM flings himself at RAY who deftly flips him past and drops him near the
desk.

RAY
(continuing)
Too bad you didn't connect. You could have gone to Juvenile Hall.
That's what you want, isn't it?

JIM
No.

RAY
Sure it is. You want to bug us till we have to lock you up. Why?

JIM
Leave me alone.

RAY
No.

JIM
I don't know why--!

RAY
Go on--don't give me that. Someone giving you hard looks?

JIM
I just get so--
(fighting tears)
Boy, sometimes the temperature goes way up.

RAY
(suddenly gentle)
Okay. Okay. Let it out.
JIM starts crying.

RAY
You feel like you want to blow your wheels right now?

JIM
All the time! I don't know what gets into me--but I keep looking for trouble and I always--I swear you better lock me up. I'm going to smash somebody--I know it.

RAY
Try the desk.
JIM smashes his fist against it, letting loose for a moment.
RAY watches, then sits near him.

RAY
That why you moved from the last town? 'Cause you were in trouble?
You can talk about it if you want to--I know about it anyway.
Routine check.

JIM
And they think they are protecting my by moving.

RAY
You were getting a good start in the wrong direction back there.
Why did you do it?

JIM
Mess that kid up?
RAY just nods.

JIM
(continuing)
He called me chicken.

RAY
And your folks didn't understand?

JIM
They never do.

RAY
So then you moved?

JIM
They think I'll make friends if we move. Just move and everything'll be roses and sunshine.

RAY
But you don't think that's a solution.
JIM is silent; he picks at his nails.

RAY
(continuing)
Things pretty tough for you at home?

JIM
She eats him alive and he takes it.
JIM stares at his family through hole in door.

JIM
What a zoo!

RAY
What?

JIM
A zoo. He always wants to be my pal, you know? But how can I give him anything when he's--I mean I love him and I don't want to hurt him--but I don't know what to do anymore except maybe die.

RAY
Pretty mixed up?

JIM
If he could--

RAY
"If he could" what? You mean your father?

JIM
I mean if he had the guts to knock
Mom cold once I bet she'd be happy and I bet she'd stop picking. They make mush out
of him. Just mush.
One thing I know is I never want to be like him.

RAY
(interrupts)
Chicken?

JIM
I bet you see right through me, don't you?
RAY shrugs.

JIM
How can anyone grow up in this circus?

RAY
You got me, Jim--but they do. Want some water?

JIM
(as RAY gets a cup of water from cooler)
Boy--if I had one day when I didn't have to be all confused and ashamed of everything-
-or I felt I belonged some place.

RAY
(giving him water)
Here. Look, will you do something for me? If the pot starts boiling again, will you come
and see me before you get yourself in a jam?
Even if you just want to talk--come in and shoot the breeze. It's easier sometimes than
talking to your folks.

JIM
Okay--

RAY
Any time--day or night. You calmed down enough to go back now?

JIM
(smiling)
You serious?
RAY smiles and opens the door.

RAY's office as JIM comes towards his MOTHER and forces himself to kiss her.

JIM
I'm sorry.

MOTHER
All right, darling.
She rises and takes his arm. They start out through the door into the hall, followed by GRANDMA and FATHER.

GRANDMA
(to RAY)
This was all very unfortunate, but he made a mistake and he's sorry-- so we're not going to have any more trouble. He's always been a lovely boy--

JIM
Lovely! Grandma--if you tell another lie you're going to turn to stone.

RAY
Luck, Jim. Don't forget.

FATHER
(offering RAY three cigars)
Have some cigars.

RAY
No thanks, I don't smoke.

FATHER
Go on--Give 'em to your friends.

RAY
No--thanks, very much, Mr. Stark.

MOTHER
Frank--he doesn't want any.
JIM grins at RAY who nods. They all leave. RAY looking after them, shakes his head and lights a cigarette. We see
JIM and his family pass through the main door. Waiting to enter, in the custody of some uniformed police, are BUZZ and the kids we saw at the opening, sullen and truculent. As they march into the lobby and JIM grows smaller in the distance, the music comes up and out.

FADE OUT.
FADE IN.

Low angle. Alley. Morning. A rabbit comes running down the alley followed by a group of young kids, screaming with pleasure.

As camera pans with the group, the littlest, a boy of five, stops near us looking after the disappearing group. The shouts of the children wane.

JUDY rushes out from a backyard beyond him. She is carrying school books and a bag lunch. She wears a polo coat against the winter wind.

JUDY
(yelling)
Beau!

The boy, who is her brother, BEAU, looks up but doesn't move.

JUDY stops at her gate. A car careens down the alley, past him.

Long shot. JUDY and BEAU seen through a window in JIM's house. JIM is in f.g. looking out through the curtains. He smiles.

JUDY
(yelling)
What are you trying to do, get yourself killed?

BEAU
(laughing)
Yes!

MOTHER (O.S.)
Your eggs are on the table, dear.

JIM turns from window and passes camera.

Full shot JIM's dining room. The MOTHER is just settling a plate of eggs at JIM's place. They FATHER is seated, drinking coffee and looking at the newspaper. GRANDMA comes in from kitchen. JIM is neatly dressed in tie, tweed jacket and slacks.

MOTHER
(continuing)
Sit down and eat--you'll be late.

JIM
(approaching table)
It'd stick in my throat, Mom. I'm nervous or something--

GRANDMA
It's a wonder we don't all have TB or some other terrible disease after living in all those smokey cities!

MOTHER
Well, drink your milk anyhow.

GRANDMA

(muttering)
There aren't so many factories here.

FATHER
Mother--

JIM
(still standing; he drinks)
You make any sandwiches?

FATHER
My first day of school, mother'd make me eat and by golly I could never even swallow
till recess--

MOTHER
(bringing bag of lunch from buffet)
There's nothing to be nervous about.
Here's peanut butter and meat loaf--
JIM makes a mouth-stuck-together-with-peanut-butter sound.

GRANDMA
What did I tell you? Peanut butter!

MOTHER
Well, there's a thermos of orange juice and some apple-sauce cake in the wax paper to
wash it down.

GRANDMA
I baked that!

JIM
(kisses her cheek)
'Bye, Mom.

MOTHER
Goodbye, dear.

FATHER
(rising)
So long, young fella. Knock 'em dead, like your old man used to!

JIM
Sure--
(gets to door and turns)
You know something? I have a feeling we're going to stay here.

FATHER
And listen--watch out about the pals you choose--Know what I mean?
Don't let them choose you--
But JIM is on his way out.
Full shot. JIM's backyard as JIM comes out of the kitchen door into the early sunshine.

JUDY (O.S.)
Come out of the alley, Beau! This is the last time I'm going to call you.
JIM blinks, pauses and sees JUDY. He takes off his tie and puts it in his pocket. Then
he starts across the backyard, camera panning with him to:
Full shot. The Alley with JIM coming out his gate, JUDY and
BEAU visible beyond. He stops again.

JUDY
Beau! All right--go to school alone!
She starts down the alley. BEAU skips after her and starts tightrope-walking the gutter
gravel.

JIM
(calling)
Hey!
JUDY glances at him briefly, but continues. JIM follows a few yards, but on his side of
the alley.

JIM
(continuing)
Hey, didn't I see you before some place?
JUDY ignores him, but something self-conscious happens to her walk. JIM runs across
the alley.
Med. shot. JUDY stopping as JIM enters. BEAU tight-rope walking on down the hill.

JIM
Hi. I saw you before.

JUDY
Bully for you.

JIM
You don't have to be unfriendly.

JUDY
Now that's true!

JIM
(smiling)
See?

JUDY
"Life is crushing in on me."

JIM
(smiling)
"Life can be beautiful." Hey, I know where it was.

JUDY
Where what was.

JIM
Where I saw you.
(no answer)
Everything going okay now?
(no answer)
You live around here?

JUDY
(relieved)
Who lives?

JIM
See, I'm new.

JUDY
Won't mother be proud.

JIM
You're really flipped--aren't you.
JUDY looks up a little surprised.

JIM
(continuing)
Where's Dawson High School?

JUDY
You going there?

JIM
Yeah--why--

JUDY
Dig the square wardrobe!

JIM

(defensively)
Yeah. So where's the high school?

JUDY
(softer)
University and 10th--Want to carry my books?
An auto horn, stuck, in the distance.

JIM
I was just getting my car. I could take you.
The horn approaches, loud.

JUDY
The kids take me.

JIM
Oh.
Another angle. JIM and JUDY as the car, horn blowing, wheels into view above them and comes careening into the alley. JUDY sees it and moves a step away from JIM.

JUDY
I'll bet you're a real yo yo.

JIM
A what?

JUDY
(yelling over horn)
Goodbye! See you!

JIM
(yelling)
I'm not so bad.
JUDY is moving toward the car.
Med. shot. Car full of kids as it comes to a jolting stop near JUDY. The boys wear suede coats, leather jackets, black peggers, boots. Their clothing is not uniform--it is the air they assume which is uniform: swaggering, self- conscious, piratical. Someone is always combing his hair.
The driver is BUZZ, whom we recognize as the leader of the stomp gang we met on Easter. He wears a leather jacket.
With him are CHICK, a slight bespectacled lad; CRUNCH,
BUZZ's first lieutenant; COOKIE, a hanger-on; GOON, a character; and the girls HELEN and MILLIE. The kids are screaming as BUZZ jams on the brakes. JUDY comes forward.
JIM hangs back.

BUZZ
Stella-a-a-a!
JUDY comes to them quickly, smiling.

JUDY
Steady Marlon!

BUZZ
Wanna make the colored lights go around and around?
JUDY and BUZZ kiss ardently and without love. JIM goes for his car.

BUZZ
(looks after JIM then at JUDY)
What's that?

JUDY
A new disease.

BUZZ
(a little suspicious)
Friend of yours?

JUDY
I'm glad they let you out.

BUZZ
Nobody chickened.

JUDY
I heard about it. You're lucky he lived.

BUZZ
They always live.
During this JIM has gotten his car and has driven up.

JIM
Where's University and 10th?

JUDY
(pointing right)
That way!

CHICK
(pointing left)
That way!

BUZZ
(pointing up)
That way!
Simultaneously, the kids laugh wildly. The radio blares.
JUDy lays her head on BUZZ's shoulder and his arm goes around her as the car zooms away. JIM looks after them a moment, then follows.

DISSOLVE TO:
Close shot. Bicycle rack. Wheels spin in, one after another and drive straight into their slots. As the nearest bike moves in:
Med. shot. PLATO just getting off his motor scooter. He comes forward, passes camera which pans with him then stops--as the school is suddenly revealed. Music starts with a crash and keeps mounting through the following.
PLATO sighs and moves away from us to join the parade of students filling the Main approach.
Parking lot as cars scream into their places noisily. JIM gets out of one and comes forward. A motorcycle roars by, just missing him. JIM stares off and starts to move as camera pans with him to:
Another angle. School. Another crash of music. JIM moves toward the parade.
Full shot. Mid-way down main approach. A number of kids pass, gossiping happily as they greet each other for the first time since vacation. Camera searches over them and stops upon our special group moving toward us--BUZZ, JUDY and the rest, all abreast. Others must park at their passage or be elbowed out of the way, staring resentfully, but not daring to challenge the group's priority. PLATO runs forward, past them.
Door from within bouncing from hand to hand as students enter. PLATO moves through the door and disappears in a milling of kids. JUDY enters with her group and moves on with them.
Med. shot. Monitor (inside corridor). The Monitor is an athletic letter-sweater boy with an arm brassard that bears the letters "HC". Kids pour past him. JIM enters.

JIM
Hi--can you tell we where I go?
I'm just starting here.

MONITOR
(pointing at brassard)
Mr. Bassett's office--203. He'll tell you where your home room is--

JIM
Thanks a lot.
JIM moves out.
Angle shot. Corridor. Shooting past a row of steel lockers.
The clash and slam of doors as kids throw in coats, pull out books and primp for the day ahead. PLATO comes to his locker, which is the nearest, and opens it.
Full shot. Corridor. JIM moves toward us from the distance.

Crowded at the entrance to a classroom in f.g. are JUDY and her pals. They are sneaking a smoke, passing the cigarette from one cupped hand to another. As JIM comes near, JUDY sees him. So do the others. They fold their arms across their chests and whistle "We are the girls of the institute"--all but JUDY. JIM glances at her and continues on past camera. A bell starts ringing crazily over the music.

Close shot. PLATO. He is straightening his tie in the mirror. Above it, pasted to the locker door, is a still of

Alan Ladd. In the mirror we can see JIM moving past. PLATO sees him too. He wheels around and stares.

PLATO
(to himself)
Hi.

The strident music of the students diminishes. The ringing of the bell stops. There remain only JIM's footsteps.

Long shot. JIM moving off down the corridor. PLATO is in f.g. looking after him. He slams his locker and starts after JIM, moving at the same speed and hovering near the wall. The footsteps of the two boys echo stonily. They are alone. JIM stops at a bulletin board near a bend in the corridor. PLATO stops too.

Bulletin board. JIM looking at the notices. PLATO drifts in several yards away and hangs near the wall watching JIM who doesn't see him. JIM reads:

Insert: Bulletin board, "Attention All Juniors and Seniors"--

Planetarium field trip--2 pm--Sharp!"

Another angle. JIM and PLATO as JIM turns from bulletin board and starts away.

PLATO
(clearing his throat)
Hi.

JIM
Hi there.

PLATO
You remember me?

JIM
No. I don't think so--

PLATO
I'm sorry--I made a mistake.

JIM starts toward camera as PLATO after another look, turns in the opposite direction and walks away from us, smashing his fist against the wall as he goes. JIM stops, full in camera. His face clouds, trying to remember. He turns full around to look after PLATO, then turns back and continues on his way. The footsteps fade.

DISSOLVE TO:

Full shot. Planetarium seen from the parking lot--a great dome crowns it--the city lies below. Camera picks up JIM's car maneuvering through the crowded lot. In b.g. a few other late-comers are dashing up steps to Planetarium. JIM drives into a small lot behind observator, parks, then runs to observatory entrance.

Full shot. Lobby as JIM runs through, opens door of theater and passes inside.

Long shot. Sky full of stars seen past JIM's head.

Darkness. This is not our sky. It is a replica of it projected onto the dome of the Planetarium. The stars slide their tentative ways in an ever-changing pattern. One of them is much larger than the rest and increases in size as we watch. Music of the spheres is heard--a high threatening tremolo.

LECTURER (O.S.)
For many days before the end of our earth people will look into the night sky and notice a star, increasingly bright and increasingly near.

JIM looks around for a seat and passes down aisle. Seen beyond him is the projector, moving slowly, its great dumb- bell head sparkling with pin-points of light. JIM takes a seat in front row. PLATO, in the row behind him, moves over a seat to be nearer. They exchange looks.

Full shot. Normal students watching intently.

LECTURER (O.S.)
As this star approaches us, the weather will change. The great polar fields of the north and south will rot and divide, and the seas will turn warmer.

Low angle. LECTURER. A dry, elderly man in a stiff white collar. He is seated at a desk, the light from the reading lamp spilling upward onto his face.

LECTURER
The last of us search the heavens and stand amazed. For the stars will still be there, moving through their ancient rhythms.

Angle shot. Students. Some watching, some taking notes.

An OLD LADY TEACHER in f.g. taps the heads of two kids in the row before her. They stop their whispering. She smiles at them.

LECTURER (O.S.)
The familiar constellations that illuminate our night will seem as they have always seemed, eternal, unchanged and little moved by the shortness of time between our planet's birth and its demise.

Med. shot. PLATO staring upward.

LECTURER (O.S.)
Orion, the Hunter.

PLATO looks off.

Med. shot. JIM (from PLATO's angle). JIM is seated in the row ahead of PLATO. His lips are parted as he looks up.

JIM

Boy!

PLATO
(leaning forward)
What?

JIM
(surprised)
Once you been up there, you know you been some place!

LECTURER (O.S.)
Gemini, the Twins.
Two shot. JUDY and BUZZ. BUZZ has his arm around her. He is nuzzling her ear. She is blandly watching the dome.

LECTURER (O.S.)
(continuing)
Cancer, the Crab.
BUZZ pokes JUDY who looks at him. He curves his wrist toward her, opening and closing his first two fingers like the pincers of a crab.

BUZZ
I'm a crab!
She laughs. So do the others.
Med. shot. JIM (PLATO behind). Seen from JUDY's angle. JIM turns at the sound of the laughter, and smiles.

LECTURER (O.S.)
Taurus, the Bull.

JIM
(in good imitation)
Moo!
He waits for approval.
Angle shot. JUDY, BUZZ and group (seen from JIM's angle).
He is in f.g. They are staring at him. Nobody laughs.

CRUNCH
(flat)
Yeah, moo.

BUZZ
Moo. That's real cute. Moo.

GOON
Hey, he's real rough--

CRUNCH
I bet he fights with cows.

BUZZ
Moo.
They turn from him. JIM withers and looks front. JUDY smiles a little and looks away
so the others cannot notice her amusement.

LECTURER (O.S.)
Sagittarius and Aries--all as they have ever been.
PLATO leans in and touches JIM's shoulder, lightly at first, then harder. JIM turns to
him.

PLATO
You shouldn't monkey with him.

JIM
What?

PLATO
He's a wheel. So's she. It's hard to make friends with them.

JIM
I don't want to make friends.
He turns back, unhappy at having revealed himself.
Another shot. JUDY, BUZZ, CRUNCH. JIM seen in b.g. The kids are whispering
among themselves and pointing at JIM, who looks up and notices. He is getting
uncomfortable.

LECTURER (O.S.)
And while the flash of our beginning has not yet traveled the light years into distance--
Full shot. The dome. The star rushes nearer, looming larger and larger. The music rises
in tension and volume.

LECTURER (O.S.)
Has not yet been seen by planets deep within the other galaxies, we will disappear into
the blackness of the space from which we came.
Two shot. JIM and PLATO staring upward, cringing back into their seats as the light
on their faces increases. Music is up loud.
Full shot. The dome seen past PLATO's head. The heavens grow brighter as the star
plummets near. Music at crescendo.

LECTURER (O.S.)
Destroyed as we began in a burst of gas and fire.

The sky is blasted by a wild flash of light. Music reaches explosion. The stars appear again.
Moving shot. Faces of normal kids watching seriously--very impressed.

LECTURER (O.S.)
(continuing)
The heavens are still and cold once more. In all the complexity of our universe and the galaxies beyond, the Earth will not be missed.
Med. shot. JIM and PLATO looking up.

LECTURER (O.S.)
Through the infinite reaches of space, the problems of Man seem trivial and naive indeed. And Man, existing alone, seems to be an episode of little consequences.
PLATO ducks his head down on the back of JIM's chair. JIM looks at him.

LECTURER (O.S.)
That's all. Thank you very much.
The lights go on. The rustle and confusion of kids stretching after sitting too long. Scattered applause. JIM rises and ruffles PLATO's hair.

JIM
Hey, it's over. The world ended.
PLATO looks up at him.

PLATO
What does he know about Man alone?
Med. shot. LECTURER as he reaches over and turns a dial.
"Morning Song" by Grieg comes on softly.
Low angle. OLD LADY TEACHER rising. She stares around at the bustling students and claps her hands sharply, but the noise is barely heard above the tumult.

TEACHER
(shrill)
May I have your attention? May I please have your attention?
Classes will meet at the busses outside. May I have your attention?
(to herself)
The heck with it.
She picks up her coat and bag.
Planetarium parking lot. School busses and autos, some new and some heaps, are parked in f.g. Beyond is the dome of the Planetarium. Kids mill about, some already driving off in their cars. One bus, already full, pulls past camera.
Mcd. shot. Front of bus seen from within. Driver in f.g.
Kids swarm up the steps and enter. PLATO is among them, but keeps looking back for JIM. PLATO boards the bus and pauses near the driver to peer through windshield. His face clouds.

Long shot. JUDY and group. Seen from PLATO's angle through windshield. They are standing idly in a loose line near
BUZZ's car. They are looking back toward Planetarium.
Med. shot. Front of bus, seen from within. PLATO turns suddenly and pushes his way past the kids who are boarding.

PLATO
Excuse me. Excuse me.
Full shot. Parking lot. Bus in f.g. Beyond it JUDY and the group are visible. PLATO squeezes out.

MALE TEACHER
John, where you going?

PLATO
I forgot something. I'll get a hitch.
PLATO moves quickly past the teacher who climbs in. The door slams, the bus moves away. PLATO stops and looks after it. The last cars are clearing the lot. Only JIM's and BUZZ's remain. PLATO looks at the small, waiting group.
Med. shot. The group seen from the rear. PLATO in the distance facing them.

BUZZ
What you looking at?
Med. shot. PLATO wild-eyed with fear.

PLATO
Nothing.
He runs off, camera panning with him. His goal is the
Planetarium Entrance, visible beyond. He races toward it frantically.
Med. shot. The group looking off after PLATO. BUZZ, nearest camera, pulls a switch-knife from his pocket and pops the long blade open. JUDY stares at it, then looks up at BUZZ apprehensively. CRUNCH sits down on the bumper and lights a cigarette.
Display lobby. Planetarium as PLATO rushes in, out of breath, stops and looks around. In distance he sees JIM leaning over the pendulum pit, smoking quietly. PLATO doesn't move. JIM hasn't even looked up.

PLATO
(screaming as if he were yelling "fire!")
What's your name!

JIM
Jim. What's yours?

PLATO
(a little quieter)
Plato. It's a nickname.

JIM nods. PLATO goes over to him, camera following, until they are close together, both leaning over the rail.

PLATO
Listen, I told you not to fool with them. Now they're waiting for you.

JIM
I know. That's why I came back.

PLATO
You scared?

JIM
I just don't want trouble.

PLATO
He has a knife.

JIM
I saw it. Gee, look at that thing swing, will you? Do you think it never stops?

PLATO
No. It's perpetual motion.

JIM
Oh, I bet some little guy comes in here at night and pushes it. Go- go-go!
PLATO walks cautiously to the door and starts outside, camera following.
Long shot. Kids (corner of Observatory) with PLATO leaning out of door, seeing them, pulling back quickly.
Inside display lobby as PLATO pulls back through the door.
JIM seems to have disappeared. PLATO stares around frightened.

PLATO
Jim?
JIM is looking at another exhibit whose mechanical voice is heard.

JIM
I'm here.

PLATO
(coming with him)
They're still there!
JIM nods. They watch the exhibit a while longer.

PLATO
Jim--Do you think when the end of the world comes it'll be at night?

JIM

No. In the morning.
PLATO looks up questioning. JIM smiles and shrugs.

JIM

I just have a feeling.
They start moving, camera leading.

PLATO

If you don't want trouble, I know a place we can go--
JIM looks up at him.

PLATO

It's a big mansion and we could sneak around there and they wouldn't even know. You could be safe--
They turn a corner quickly.
Doors to balcony (from inside) as JIM and PLATO come to them from behind camera, fling the doors open and step outside.
Balcony as JIM and PLATO come onto it, lean on the parapet.
PLATO points off.

PLATO

There it is.
High long shot. Mansion. (Matte). It is falling into elegant ruin, casting long afternoon shadows on the great lawns and promenades.
Closeup PLATO looking urgently at JIM.

PLATO

Should we go?
Two shot. JIM and PLATO. PLATO's back is to us. JIM looks past him and sees something.

JIM

(quietly)
The shadows are getting long.
PLATO turns to look too.
Long high shot. Parking lot. JIM's car is where he left it.
Into the driveway, like logs driven before a sea, the shadows of the waiting kids appear and advance until the kids themselves come into view. They pause there a moment, then look up.

HELEN

(smiling)
Le soleil tombe dans la mer.

Laughter. The kids scatter along the wall at the foot of the balcony stairs. BUZZ goes to JIM's car, knife in hand, and stands silently.

Low angle. Two shot. JIM and PLATO staring down from balcony parapet. At last JIM moves out past camera.

Low angle. Long shot. JIM and PLATO. JUDY in f.g. The two boys walk down the stairs. Camera pans with them as they reach parking lot level and start walking past other members of the group.

Traveling shot. JIM and PLATO coming forward.

Dolly shot. BUZZ from JIM's angle. As camera moves in toward BUZZ standing alone at the car, he suddenly bends down and slashes JIM's tire. Camera stops. There is the hiss of air escaping. BUZZ straightens and smiles past camera.

Close shot. JIM inhaling sharply in shock and suppressed anger.

Full shot over JIM's car. Group in b.g. motionless. JIM and PLATO approach the car. JIM stops and looks down. BUZZ stands smiling and puts away the knife.

Close shot. Rear wheel. The tire slashed, the wheel rests on the ground.

Full shot. Car. Shooting between group and BUZZ toward backs of JIM and PLATO, who are looking down at car which rests on its rims. JIM turns and moves toward group. He stops, looks from one to the other and smiles nervously.

Then he looks straight at BUZZ.

JIM
(wearily)
You know something?

BUZZ
What?

JIM
(reproachfully)
You watch too much television.

Med. shot. The group and JIM. JUDY has come to BUZZ, stands on the wall above him.

BUZZ
Hey, he's real abstract and different.

JIM
I'm cute, too.

Suddenly GOON starts clucking softly like a chicken. One by one the others pick it up. BUZZ, the last, crows. Silence.

Med. shot. The group and JIM.

JIM
Meaning me?

BUZZ

What?

JIM
Chicken?
The group gives a quick, short laugh.
Med. shot. JIM as he takes off his glasses, smiles. Shakes his head disapprovingly.

JIM
You shouldn't call me that.
Close shot. PLATO watching anxiously.
Med. shot. BUZZ with JUDY watching above him. JIM enters shot until he is close to BUZZ's face. He looks up at JUDY.
Camera closes in until we are tight on the three. The heads are nearly touching.

JIM
(softly to JUDY)
You always at ringside? You always travel in this rank company?
BUZZ clutches JIM's hair and jerks his head up. He cracks
JIM smartly across the face with the palm of his hand.
Close shot. JUDY looking at JIM. Her eyes clear in recognition.
Another angle. The group and JIM as JIM tears free and comes at BUZZ, slugging. But BUZZ, with a laugh, leaps onto the parapet and turns, the knife in his hand again. JIM stops short. The group and PLATO move in around him.

JIM
I thought only punks fought with knives.

BUZZ
Who's fighting? This is the test, man. It's a crazy game.

HELEN
Les jeux de courage!
Close-up. CRUNCH. He is smiling. His arms are around the shoulders of the kids who flank him.

CRUNCH
(wetting his lips)
Machismo. Machismo.
Med. shot. Group.

JIM
Machismo?

BUZZ
Somebody find him a knife.
Close shot. PLATO seen between heads of MIL and COOKIE.

COOKIE holds up a switch knife and tosses it over into the circle.

PLATO
Jim!
Full shot. Circle as the knife falls at JIM's feet. JIM stoops and picks up his weapon,
then faces BUZZ. Then he springs his blade.

BUZZ
You know the action? No cutting.
Just sticking--jab real cool.
BUZZ hops from the parapet. They begin stalking each other.
BUZZ slides his knife from hand to hand trying to hypnotize
JIM. Suddenly he pokes out and pricks JIM's shirt. The group sighs "Ole!" JIM makes
no effort at self-defense.
Silence. BUZZ pricks JIM again, "Ole!"

BUZZ
(as he maneuvers)
What you waiting on, Toreador? I thought you wanted some action!
JIM cuts out half-heartedly.

BUZZ
Big brave bull. Hah! Toro! Hah!
Hah!

GOON
Moo!

BUZZ
Come on--Fascinate us. Impress us.
What's happening? Let's go!

JIM
I don't want trouble.

BUZZ
(furious suddenly)
You crud chicken! You're wasting our time!
BUZZ viciously slaps JIM across the face. JIM lashes out and misses. BUZZ hops back.

BUZZ
Yeah--that's pretty close. How about a little closer, Toreador?
Cut off a button and you get to join the club!
Outside entrance of parking lot. A uniformed GUIDE of middle-age stares past camera.
Cries of "Ole," are heard in the distance.

GUIDE
(turning)
Mr. Minton! Mr. Minton! Trouble!
The LECTURER appears running. He stops short at what he sees, and blinks in the sunlight.

GUIDE
Look. There's your audience.

LECTURER
Oh, I don't think so. From the school?
Inside circle. JIM is covered with sweat and about to drop.
He is getting the worst of it, still refusing to defend himself.
Close shot. PLATO. He is looking on in despair.

GROUP
Ole! Ole!
Suddenly, with a cry, PLATO pushes through.
Inside circle as PLATO comes through. His eyes are wild.
He holds a tire chain in his hand.

MIL
Buzzy! Look out! He's got a chain!

BUZZ
(smiling as he sees PLATO)
Hey! Chicken Little!
BUZZ trips PLATO quickly and kicks him while he's down.
CRUNCH grabs the chain.

JIM
All right--you want it, you got it!
Suddenly JIM transforms. He bores forward expertly--pricks
BUZZ again and again. Cries of Ole greet him. BUZZ is surprised.
Full shot. Group. We hear only the breathing of the combatants. Beyond we see the GUIDE approaching swiftly.
The LECTURER trails at a safe distance.
Closeup. CRUNCH. He looks up. His smile fades.

CRUNCH
Honk. Let's split.
Group as they look off and see the GUIDE and LECTURER approach. BUZZ and JIM are both breathing hard. PLATO is getting to his feet.

BUZZ
Split for what? Couple old poopheads?

He folds up his knife and puts it away. So does JIM.

JIM
You satisfied or you want more?

BUZZ
How 'bout you? Say the word and you're cold, Jack--you're dead.

JUDY
Buzzie--we better get out of here.

BUZZ
What's eating you, Judy? You want him alive?

JIM
Where can we meet?

BUZZ
Know the Millertown bluff?

COOKIE
The bluff, Buzz! That's dangerous up there.

BUZZ
Draw him a picture, Chicken Little.
Eight o'clock. Cookie, you call
Moose and get a couple cars. We're going to have us some real kicks.
Little chickie-run. You been on chickie-runs before?

JIM
Sure--that's all I do.
The GUIDE bursts in among them. The LECTURER remains on the fringe.

GUIDE
All right--all of you--start moving!

JUDY
You mean l'il ol' us? What's the matter with the nice man?

GUIDE
Don't clown with me.

BUZZ
Why'nt you go suck on something sweet?

GUIDE

You think you're tough? I got a son twice your size and I can still handle him.

LECTURER
Don't lose control, Mr. Jamison. I think if we just explain--

GUIDE
Explain to these? They think they own the world!

CRUNCH
The world is round!

MIL
The world is flat!

COOKIE
All the world's a stage!
There is wild laughter from the kids as they close around the GUIDE and start edging him away, up the steps toward the
Planetarium balcony.

KIDS
The world goes round the sun!
Goodbye proud world!
I got the world on a string!
The world's my oyster!
Hey! A fish-eater! Brain food.
They are gone. The LECTURER looks after them then comes to
JIM. JIM looks down at his shirt. There are spots of blood.
PLATO opens it, spits on a handkerchief and starts to wipe the blood away.

LECTURER
(smiling wanly, to JIM)
Sometimes the world is too much with us, isn't it, son? What was the disturbance?

JIM
Nothing.

LECTURER
You're bleeding. Are you all right?

JIM
I scratched my mosquito bites. I'm fine.
LECTURER hesitates.

JIM
I'm fine--thanks!

LECTURER goes. JIM impatiently closes his shirt.

PLATO
Are you really going to meet them?

JIM
Who knows. Plato?

PLATO
What?

JIM
What's a chickie-run?

DISSOLVE TO:
Downstairs hall. JIM's house. A single light is burning.
JIM steals in from the kitchen, peers cautiously into the living room, then starts up the stairs. A crash is heard above. JIM stops, undecided whether to go or stay, then moves quickly up the stairs, no longer trying to be quiet.
Upper hall. JIM's house as JIM rises into view at the top of stairs. He sees a figure on hands and knees mopping something off the rug. Leaklight from the staircase dims details. An apron is tied around the figure's waist and its bow sticks bravely in the air.

JIM
Mom?
The figure straightens and turns around, smiling. It is the
FATHER. He is neatly dressed in his business suit but wears a Mary Petty apron.

FATHER
Hiya, Jimbo.
JIM leans against the wall, shaking his head and trying not to laugh. The FATHER laughs unhappily, trying to make it all seem a joke.

FATHER
You thought I was Mom?

JIM
Yeah!

FATHER
It's just this get-up. The girl's out and I was bringing Mom's supper.

JIM
(giggling)
And you dropped it?

FATHER
(laughing too)
Yeah! Shh!

JIM
That's funny!

FATHER
I better clean this up before she sees it.
He starts dabbing among the spilled dishes with a wet cloth.
JIM watches him.

JIM
Let her see. What could happen.
The FATHER continues dabbing.

JIM
Dad--
The FATHER looks up at him.

JIM
Dad--don't. Don't.
JIM touches his FATHER's elbow, bringing him to his feet.
They look at each other a moment then JIM goes to his bedroom. The FATHER goes
back to mopping up the mess.
Inside JIM's room as he comes in, shuts the door and throws himself miserably on his
bed. He writhes as if the pain he feels were physical. Outside, radios are heard in the
night--tuned to different stations. He feels under his jacket and holds up his hand to the
moonlight. There is blood on it. He reaches up and takes his alarm clock and is setting
it as camera glides to his window and holds over the rooftops.
Full shot. JUDY's backyard. Moonlight. JUDY stands near camera looking up at the
moon. The radios seem louder out here. One breaks through.

ANNOUNCER
Time now for the seven o'clock news.
Friends, the next time you go shopping.

JUDY'S FATHER (O.S.)
Judy.
She wheels around.
Long shot. The FATHER standing erect on back porch, silhouetted against a window.

JUDY'S FATHER
What are you wishing for, Judy?
Med. shot. JUDY. She hasn't moved.

JUDY
(softly)
I wasn't wishing. I was looking at the moon.
Full shot. Backyard featuring the FATHER. We see him now as a tall and handsome
man. There is something boyish and appealing about him.

JUDY'S FATHER
(singing lightly)
"Man in the Moon, how came you there--
Up in the sky where you are shining--
Floating so high in the frosty air--?
Oh, say--Man in the Moon!"--
JUDY comes forward, stands below him on the step. Her look is adoring.

JUDY
(astonished)
How did you know that?

JUDY'S FATHER
We used to sing it in school.
(smiles)
Don't look at me with such horror.
They had schools in those days.

JUDY
But the same song. I think it's fantastic!

JUDY'S FATHER
We were romantic then too--

JUDY
Are you and Mom home tonight?

JUDY'S FATHER
No. Why?

JUDY
Nothing, only it'd be nice to spend an evening together for a change.

JUDY'S FATHER
With us old creeps? Come on, we have to eat.

JUDY
(rising)
Daddy--
He looks at her.

JUDY
Good evening.

JUDY'S FATHER
Hi.
He turns away and goes into the house. She hesitates and then follows. Something in the moods has changed. He has neglected to hold the door for her.
Dining room. JUDY's house as the FATHER comes to the head of the table and takes his seat. Three places are set.
JUDY follows. She stands above his chair, looking down at him as he drinks his tomato juice.

JUDY
(quietly, afraid)
Didn't you forget something?

JUDY'S FATHER
What?
JUDY doesn't answer, but leans down and kisses him quickly on the lips.

JUDY'S FATHER
(continuing; shocked)
What's the matter with you?
JUDY freezes, frightened. He collects himself a little.

JUDY'S FATHER
(continuing)
You're too old for that kind of stuff, kiddo. I thought you stopped doing that long ago.

JUDY
(very hurt)
I didn't want to stop.
The mother enters briskly from another part of the house--an attractive, brittle woman of thirty-five.

JUDY'S MOTHER
Didn't want to stop what?

JUDY'S FATHER
Nothing.

JUDY
I was talking to Dad.

JUDY'S FATHER

I didn't kiss her so it's a big thing.

JUDY'S MOTHER
(calling to kitchen)
Bertha! You can serve the souffle!
(to FATHER)
Fish souffle.
(to JUDY)
You don't have to stand there, darling. Drink your tomato juice.
JUDY slides into her chair reluctantly and unfolds her napkin.

JUDY
I guess I just don't understand anything.

JUDY'S FATHER
I'm tired, Judy. I'd like to change the subject.

JUDY
Why?

JUDY'S FATHER
I'd like to, that's all. Girls your age don't do that. You need an explanation?

JUDY
(very low)
Girls don't love their father?
Since when? Since I got to be sixteen?
She half-rises to kiss him again.

JUDY'S FATHER
Stop it now! Sit down!
Suddenly the FATHER slaps her. Even as he does it he is as stunned as JUDY. The mother stops eating. She has never seen such a display and is shocked. He tries to control himself by buttering a piece of bread. There is a terrible silence into which BEAU enters in his pajamas. He runs to his FATHER's chair, then halts--looking from face to face. The FATHER puts an arm around him, hugs him almost savagely.

JUDY'S FATHER
(thickly)
Hi, rascal.

BEAU
(hushed)
Hi.
JUDY rises, weeping.

JUDY
May I please be excused?
She starts out. The FATHER rises and follows after her.

JUDY'S FATHER
(softly)
Hey, hey, Glamorpuss. I'm sorry.
She leaves the room, interrupting the joke he was going to make. He turns back to the table and sits down. The MOTHER rises and comes to him.

JUDY'S FATHER
(continuing)
I don't know what to do. All of a sudden she's a problem.
The mother stands behind his chair. She tips his head back against her body and kneads his neck and shoulders.

JUDY'S MOTHER
She'll outgrow it, dear. It's just the age.

BEAU
(in a sudden burst)
The atomic age!
The door slams.

JUDY'S MOTHER
(kissing her husband's hair)
It's the age when nothing fits.
Inside JIM's room. We see him lying on his bed as before.
His eyes are open. The alarm clock goes off. JIM starts as if shot, then stops the wild ringing. The time is seven- forty-five. He makes no move to leave the bed. There is a light tap on the door, then it opens and the FATHER is there, seen in light from the hall and still wearing the apron.

FATHER
You awake?

JIM
Yes.

FATHER
Listen--I took a steak out of the freezer. I thought we could have a real old-fashioned stag party--just the two of us, what do you say?

JIM
I'm not hungry.
The FATHER turns away.

JIM
Hey--I want to ask you something.

FATHER
(happily)
Shoot, Jimbo.

JIM
Suppose you knew that you had to do something very dangerous--where you have to
prove something you need to know--a question of honor. Would you do it?

FATHER
(laughing)
Is there some kind of trick answer?

JIM
What would you do, Dad?

FATHER
(evading)
I wouldn't do anything hasty.
Let's get a little light on the subject.
The FATHER turns on the light and looks at JIM who is now sitting on the edge of the
bed. He removes his jacket and the bloody shirt is revealed. The FATHER stares.

JIM
Blood.

FATHER
How'd that happen! What kind of trouble you in?

JIM
The kind we've been talking about.
Can you answer me now?

FATHER
Listen--nobody should make a snap decision--This isn't something you just--we ought
to consider all the pros and cons--

JIM
We don't have time.

FATHER
We'll make time. Where's some paper. We'll make a list and if we're still stuck then we
ought to get some advice--

He goes out, to the study next door. JIM rises.

JIM
What can you do when you have to be a man?

FATHER
Well, now--

JIM
Just give me a direct answer!
(pause)
You going to stop me from going, Dad?

FATHER
You know I never stop you from anything. Believe me--you're at a wonderful age. In ten years you'll look back on this and wish you were a kid again.

JIM
Ten years? Now, Dad--I need an answer now!

FATHER
I just want to show you how foolish you are. When you're older you'll laugh at yourself for thinking this is so important--
During this, JIM has kicked off his shoes and put on his boots and jacket and goes out. Living room featuring stairs. JIM comes running down the stairs and out the kitchen door.

FATHER (O.S.)
Jim? Will you listen? You can't go out till we--Jim!
The FATHER comes down the stairs, goes to the front door and calls:

FATHER
Jim? Jim!
He goes to kitchen door, calls again, gets no answer, comes back into the living room, sees he is still wearing the apron. He rips it off and throws it down--then starts for the stairs.

DISSOLVE TO:
The Plateau. Moonlight. Wind shrieks over the exposed plateau, which is several hundred yards long. It cuts into the darkness like the prow of a ship and ends in empty air.
A dozen cars are scattered about, defining a sort of runway in the center. There are twenty kids present, but very little talk. Most of them belong to BUZZ's group but there are a few whom we have not met before. They stand in small clots, murmuring and smoking. The atmosphere is strung tightly, like the moments before a dawn attack. In b.g. near the cliff's edge, are two cars of similar make and model. They face away from

camera toward the edge of the plateau. There are no headlights anywhere...blackout conditions.

MOOSE, a boy in a leather jacket and cheap yachting cap stands guard between the cars, his back to us. His hands are on his hips. His legs are spread. Some girls drift in. Another angle. Plateau featuring PLATO as he wanders through the crowd searching for JIM. He passes BUZZ's car where BUZZ, JUDY and the rest are eating hamburgers. They have all changed into fighting wardrobe.

BUZZ
(calling out)
Hey, Chicken-Little.
PLATO stops.

BUZZ
Where's Toreador? He beg off?

PLATO
He's not scared of you.

BUZZ
(laughing)
Yeah?
(to GOON)
Goon! You seen that adolescent type anywheres?

COOKIE
He won't show.

GOON
Well, you going to wait all night?
I'm getting nervous, man! We got to do something!

CRUNCH
(looking off)
Hey, Buzz!

BUZZ
What?

COOKIE
Over there.
BUZZ snaps on the spotlight again and swings it off.
Full shot. JIM's car as JIM gets out and PLATO runs to him.

JIM
How'd you get here?

PLATO
I hitched.

JIM
Boy, I bet you'd go to a hanging.

PLATO
My personality's showing again.
Should I leave?

JIM
No. It's okay.
BUZZ enters.

BUZZ
Come on. Let's see what we're driving.
JIM gets out; PLATO starts to follow.

BUZZ
Just him.

JIM
Stay there.
The two boys move away. PLATO looks after them, hurt, then goes to side of JUDY
and stands.
Dolly shot. JIM and BUZZ as they come forward.

BUZZ
What you say your name was?

JIM
Jim Stark.

BUZZ
Buzz Gundersen.

JIM
Hi.

BUZZ
Glad to meet you.
They shake hands briefly as they walk. They come to MOOSE and stop.

MOOSE
Got some goodies for you, Buzzie-boy.

We got to do something. Don't we?
Long shot. JIM and BUZZ with PLATO in f.g. JIM and BUZZ appear to him as two close friends. Suddenly they break and go, without speaking further, to their cars. They back up to the opposite end of the plateau, headlights dark. PLATO follows them with his gaze.
Group shot. GOON and others looking up as the cars glide by.
Med. shot. JUDY waiting as BUZZ and JIM move into starting position next to her. JUDY goes to BUZZ. JIM is in b.g.-- looking on.

JUDY
Feel okay?

BUZZ
Give me some dirt.
She bends out of sight for a moment as BUZZ goes on talking, then hands him the dirt. He rubs it into his palms.

BUZZ
Hey, Toreador! She signals. We head for the edge. The first guy who jumps--chicken!
JUDY and BUZZ kiss, without much interest.

BUZZ
What's happening?

JUDY
Good luck, Buzz.
She starts out, without kissing him again.

JIM
(calling softly)
Judy.
Med. shot. JIM's car as JUDY comes to him.

JIM
Me too.
She looks at him a moment then bends and hands him some dirt.
Their heads touch for an instant.

JIM
Thank you.
She breaks the look and hurries away.
Long shot. The cars. They are lined up in two rows-- headlights facing each other. JUDY comes into shot. When she gets near camera, she stops and turns back to face them.

BUZZ
Hit your lights!

Suddenly the headlights of all the cars come on full.

Reverse shot. JUDY. She is in the center of the glare.

Behind her we see the other kids filing out of their cars, hurrying toward the edge of the bluff. The sound of the two motors revving then dying and revving again.

Inside JIM's car. JIM grips the wheel firmly, relaxes his hands to rub his palms together and crack his knuckles. He grips the wheel again. Steps on the accelerator, winding his engine into a roar. He lets up, looks tensely at--

BUZZ in his car. His chin juts forward. He lets go of the wheel, starts to comb his hair.

Slow pan shot. Spectators staring off at the cars. A boy has his arm around the girl in front of him, his cheek against hers. Both are looking off. Some of the kids smoke. All are involved in the blasting of engines.

PLATO among the spectators near edge of the bluff. He is chewing his lip. Camera pans down to show that the fingers of both his hands are tightly crossed.

Close shot. JUDY staring tensely into the glare. Suddenly she raises her hands high above her head.

Close shot. JIM sweating it out. He leans forward, squinting, ready.

Close shot. BUZZ. He puts his comb between his teeth and clamps it hard. He settles himself for the run.

Long shot. Plateau. The cars are in close, seen from the rear. JUDY is a small distant figure, arms stretched high.

The exhaust blasts. Now she drops her arms. The cars leap ahead.

Med. shot. JUDY. She whirls to see the cars snap by, then begins running up the center of the plateau between the lines of spectators.

Full shot. Spectators. Shooting over their shoulders as the cars approach and scream past.

Pit shot. Cars. As they approach, gaining speed, and thunder over the camera.

Inside JIM's car. (Process). He is tense.

Inside BUZZ's car. (Process). His hands hard on the wheel.

The comb is still between his teeth. He begins edging toward the door on his left.

Moving close shot. JUDY biting hard on her finger, as she runs forward.

Close shot. PLATO. Both hands cover his mouth. The fingers are still crossed.

Inside JIM's car. (Process). As he edges to his left. He is driving with one hand. He opens the door, gets set for his jump.

Inside BUZZ's car. (Process). He reaches for the door handle and misses. As he raises his arm to reach again, the strap of his windbreaker sleeve slips over the handle. He looks down in panic, then back at the drop ahead. He tugs but cannot get the sleeve loose.

Closeup. PLATO staring. He shuts his eyes tight and keeps them shut.

Shooting at backs of the two cars as they race through the row of lights toward the edge.

Inside JIM's car. (Process). His face is soaked. He looks once toward BUZZ--then ahead. His eyes widen in fear. He shoves left and flings himself forward, and out.

Outside JIM's car as he sprawls forward--into camera.

Inside BUZZ's car. (Process). BUZZ leans way forward now.

He seems to rise in his seat. His mouth opens and the comb falls out.

Full shot spectators staring in disbelief. Suddenly a youth ducks his face into the neck of his girlfriend so he cannot see. At the same instant--

CROWD
(in a single breath)
Oh!
Rear view. Edge of the bluff as the two cars go over.
There is NO human sound.
Close shot. JIM as he stops rolling.
BUZZ's car in flight. (Special effects). The car soars through the night, the vehicle of a terrible journey.
Med. shot. BUZZ. (Process). Surprise has gone. He rides lightly on the thrill of his last moment--then suddenly, his face twists in a spasm of protest and loss.
The kids staring at his flight.
JIM unaware of the disaster--glad he made it.
Low angle. Edge of the bluff. With headlights blazing, both cars dive down.
Med. shot. JUDY standing frozen as the spectators shove past and around her.
Wide angle. Edge of the bluff as spectators swarm to it, stand looking down.
JIM on hands and knees, trying to rise. Legs rush by him, knock him onto his face.
Long shot. (Special effects). Both cars plunge into the ocean below.
JIM at edge of bluff. He is pushing through spectators.

JIM
(a harsh whisper)
Where's Buzz! Where's Buzz!
PLATO working his way through the crowd.

PLATO
(calling)
Jim! Jim!
CRUNCH. CRUNCH looks up as he hears JIM's repeated cry.
JIM enters behind him, continuing blindly on his way.

CRUNCH
(tight fury)
Down there! Down there is Buzz!
JIM looks over the edge.
Rear view. Spectators. A siren wail approaches. The kids wheel and scatter, panicking past the camera.
Close shot. MOOSE. Looks at JIM. Runs.
Close shot. GOON. Turns. Runs.
Med. shot. JIM seen between legs of hurrying kids. The sirens and the pounding of their feet on the hard turf. JIM is sitting on the edge of the bluff. PLATO rushes in, stops short as he sees him.

PLATO
Come on, Jim! We got to get out of here!
JIM doesn't move. PLATO grabs his arm and yanks.

PLATO

Get up! Get up! Come on!
JIM stands. PLATO pushes him.

PLATO

Go on! Move!
They start away, PLATO still pushing from behind.
Med. shot. JUDY. She is standing alone in the wind on the emptying plateau. JIM and
PLATO move past in the distance.
JIM sees her and stops.
Close shot. JUDY. She is shuddering violently but there are no tears. She seems not to
see or hear or be aware of anything around her.
Full shot. JIM and PLATO watching JUDY. JIM moves toward her, camera panning
with him and leaving PLATO behind. JIM stands before JUDY until she notices him.
He shakes his head for all the sorrow he feels, but no words come.
Tentatively he offers her his hand. After a moment, she takes it. She knows only that
help is being offered and that she will accept it with trust. JIM leads her away toward
the car.

DISSOLVE TO:

High long shot. JIM's street. Night. There is no movement anywhere. In the house
bordering the street a few lights still burn. JIM's car approaches out of distance and
slows when it reaches the alley.
Med. shot. JIM's car as it slows and stops. JIM, JUDY and
PLATO in the front seat. JUDY has the door open before the car even stops. She is
shaking, agitated and withdrawn.

JUDY

(hardly audible)
This is fine--
She gets out and starts away, leaving door open.

JIM

(calling quietly)
Judy. Will you be okay?
PLATO looks at him. JUDY hesitates. JIM raises a hand to her in a shy farewell. She
smiles vaguely, then hurries away from them.
Near JIM's backyard (alley). JIM and PLATO.

JIM

I got to go in. You better get home too.
(touches PLATO)
Hey--what?

PLATO

Why don't you come home with me? I mean nobody's home at my house--and
I'm not tired, are you? I don't have many--people I can talk to.

JIM
Who has?

PLATO
If you want to come we could talk and then in the morning we could have breakfast like
my dad used to--
(pauses--then excitedly as though an idea had suddenly struck him)
Gee...if you could only have been my father...we could...

JIM
(interrupting)
Hey...you flipped--or something?
You better take off...

PLATO
(suddenly, pleasantly)
O.K. G'night. I got to pick up my scooter. See you tomorrow.

JIM
Yeah.
PLATO turns, walks up the alley to the street. JIM goes into his kitchen door.
Hallway. JUDY's house. Three doors open onto it: one is closed--this is JUDY's room:-
-another, leading into BEAU's room is open, but the room beyond is dark: the third, also
open, reveals the bedroom of JUDY's parents. As JUDY comes into the hallway, the
parents, who are reading in their beds, look up. JUDY hesitates, then starts toward her
own room.

BEAU (O.S.)
(quietly)
Hello, little cute sister.
JUDY stops. BEAU appears at his door in white pajamas, a small ghost. JUDY looks
at him.

BEAU
Hello, darling, baby-pie, glamor- puss, sweetie--
JUDY touches BEAU's head and tries to smile.

JUDY'S FATHER
(calling from his bed)
Beau! You belong in bed!
BEAU flees. JUDY turns without another glance at her parents, and opens the door of
her room.

Inside bedroom of JUDY's parents. As JUDY slams her bedroom door o.s., the FATHER reacts. Perhaps, he wishes she had given him a chance to say goodnight. The MOTHER, who use reading glasses, looks up at the slam. Then she looks over at her husband, shrugs when she catches his gaze, and goes back to her magazine.
Inside JIM's living room. The television is on, but only a hum comes from it, and the screen is a flickering gray. The
FATHER sits lumpily in a chair by the fireplace, still dressed but with his collar open. The sound of JIM's step in the dining room makes him open his eyes. Fear of facing his son makes him shut them again. The boy comes in, a bottle of milk in his hand. Seeing his FATHER there, he stops short--his impulse is to flee. Instead he comes in and looks down at the sleeping man whose eyelids, fluttering in the FATHER's masquerade of sleep, make him seem to be having a dream. JIM is torn between his desire to leave and his need to speak. He turns off the television quietly, then lies down on the couch across the way. He mumbles the things he would say to his FATHER and the answers he feels he would get. The old man opens his eyes once, sees the boy there, head banging upside down from the couch. Then he shuts them again.
Upside down long shot. Room (JIM's viewpoint). Suddenly, inverted in his vision, the MOTHER appears at the head of the stairs, in bathrobe and nightgown. She pauses a moment, then runs down crying:

MOTHER
He's home! You're home! You're all right!
The camera rights itself suddenly.
JIM as he completes his turn, pulling his head up and sitting.
FATHER as he pretends to awaken with a start.
Full shot, room as the MOTHER hurries to JIM, holds him, inspects him, kisses him.

MOTHER
What happened, darling. We were so worried. I was going to take a sleeping pill, but I wouldn't till
I knew you were home.

JIM
I have to talk to someone, Mom. I have to talk to you both. And Dad this time you got to give me an answer.

FATHER
Go ahead.

JIM
I'm in terrible trouble.--You know that big high bluff near Miller- town Junction?

FATHER
Sure--there was a bad accident there. They showed the pictures on

T.V.

JIM
I was in it.

MOTHER
How!

JIM
It doesn't matter how. I was driving a stolen car--

MOTHER
Do you enjoy doing this to me or what--

JIM
Mom--I'm not--

MOTHER
And you wanted him to make a list!

FATHER
Will you let him tell it!

JIM
She never wants to hear. She doesn't care!

MOTHER
I guess when I nearly died giving birth to you--that shows how much I don't care!

FATHER
Just relax, please relax!

JIM
I told you Dad, it was a question of honor. They called me chicken-- you know, chicken!
I had to go or
I would never have been able to face any of those kids again. So I got in one of these
cars and a boy called Buzz got in the other. We had to drive fast and jump before the
cars went over the edge of the bluff. I got out okay but Buzz didn't. He was killed.

MOTHER
Good Lord!

JIM
I can't keep it to myself anymore--

FATHER
Well, just get it off your chest, son.

JIM
That's not what I mean. I've never done anything right. I've been going around with my head in a sling for years...I don't want to drag you into this but I can't help it. I don't think I can prove anything by going around pretending
I'm tough any more, so maybe you look like one thing but you still feel like another.

FATHER
You're absolutely right!

JIM
Are you listening to me? You're involved in this! I want to go to the police and tell them I was mixed up in this thing tonight?

FATHER
You what?

MOTHER
No!

FATHER
Did anyone see you there? I mean did they get your license number or anything?

JIM
I don't think so--

FATHER
Well--

MOTHER
What about the other boys--Do you think they'll go to the police?

JIM
What's that got to do with it?

MOTHER
Why should you be the only one.

FATHER
Look Jim. Far be it from me to tell you what to do, but there's--

MOTHER
Are you going to preach now? Are we going to have a sermon?

FATHER
I'm just explaining what you mean!
You can't be an idealist all your life! Nobody thanks you for sticking your neck out!

MOTHER
That's right!

JIM
Except yourself!

FATHER
Will you wait a minute?

JIM
You don't want me to go.

MOTHER
No! I don't want you to go to the police! There were other people and why should you
be the only one involved!

JIM
But I am involved! We're all involved, Mom! A boy was killed!
I don't see how we can get out of that by pretending it didn't happen!

FATHER
You know you did wrong. That's the main thing, isn't it?

JIM
No! It's nothing! Just nothing!
You always told me to tell the truth. You think you can just turn that off?

MOTHER
He's not saying that! He's saying don't volunteer!

JIM
Just tell a little white lie?

FATHER
You'll learn as you get a little older, Jim.

JIM
I don't want to learn that!

MOTHER
Well, it doesn't matter anyhow-- because we're moving.

JIM
No! You're not tearing me loose any more.

MOTHER
Do I have to spell it out?

JIM
You're not going to use me as an excuse again, Mom. Every time you can't face yourself you want to move and you say it's because of me or the neighborhood or some other phony excuse. Now I want to do one thing right and I'm not letting you run away.
(silence)
Dad?

FATHER
Son--this is all happening so fast--

JIM
You better give me something, Dad.
You better give me something
(stops as he sees the emptiness in them)
Mom?

MOTHER
Jimmy, you're very young--and a foolish decision now could wreck your whole life.

JIM
Dad--answer her--aren't you going to stand up for me?
The FATHER is mute, helpless... Suddenly JIM screams.

JIM
Dad?
He leaps at his FATHER, dragging him to his feet, hands at the man's throat.

MOTHER
Stop it! You'll kill him! Jim!
Do you want to kill your father?
Suddenly JIM loosens his hands and rises. He looks swiftly at each of them--moves a few steps toward the door, looks back at them again--then rushes out of the house. The parents stand frozen.

DISSOLVE TO:
Outside Precinct Station. JIM's car comes to a stop at the curb. JIM gets out and approaches the flight of steps leading up the entrance. A bare bulb on either side is the only illumination. As he mounts the first step, the double doors above him swing open revealing several people. JIM stops short. So do they.
Low angle. CRUNCH, MOOSE and their parents. JIM's back in f.g. The boys stare down at him.
High angle. JIM (from the boys' point of view) as he stares up at them. MOOSE's father takes his arm and starts him down the stairs, the others moving too.

MOOSE
Let go of me--

MOOSE'S FATHER
You want a good crack in the mouth?
JIM starts forward up the steps. CRUNCH grabs him.

CRUNCH
This place appeal to you or something?
They move down the steps as JIM breaks away and continues up.
He goes through the doors.
Inside doors as JIM comes through and stops. He looks back through the glass. We see
the group reach the curb where their cars are parked. There is a brief discussion which
we cannot hear, then CRUNCH and MOOSE move off to MOOSE's car.
JIM turns back. He looks worried as he passes camera.
Med. shot. CRUNCH and MOOSE. They stop at MOOSE's car and look back at the
entrance. The parents are seen beyond them, getting into their cars. CRUNCH is near
tears with anger.

CRUNCH
What's he going to pull--

MOOSE
Nothing, Crunch. They picked him up like the rest of--

CRUNCH
You see any cops?

MOOSE'S FATHER
(yelling)
You monsters start home. We're going to--

MOOSE
Yeah. Yeah.

MOOSE'S FATHER
We're following you so better get there.

CRUNCH
You see any cops?

MOOSE
No--

CRUNCH

He's going to cheese, I tell you.
Nobody arrested him!

MOOSE
I think I should go home.

CRUNCH
No. We're going to bring him down.

MOOSE
Crunch--my father's--You going to kill him?

CRUNCH
(crying)
You clean out of your head? Come on!
CRUNCH gets into the car. MOOSE follows. They gun the motor and throw the car into a sharp U-turn. MOOSE'S FATHER jumps into his car. He steps on the starter but nothing happens--just the empty whirring, over and over. Finally it starts, but the boys have gone.
Inside Precinct Station. Juvenile division. A desk sergeant is writing in the record book. Facing him across the desk and handcuffed to an officer is a young hoodlum, very different in appearance from the kids we have met--a typical duck-tail 'cat'.

SERGEANT
(spelling)
W-O-J-T-what?

HOODLUM
O-W-I-C-Z. Wojtowicz. What's the matter, man? That's the craziest name in town! It swings!

JIM
Excuse me--but--You know where I can find--I mean I don't remember his last name--

SERGEANT
Look--can't you see I'm writing?

HOODLUM
(combing his duck-tail)
Man, this cat never stops. He just keeps going like Big Jay at a session!

OFFICER
Shut up.

HOODLUM
He's writing a book about me--

SERGEANT
What I could write about you they wouldn't print.

JIM
I think his first name's Ray--I have to see him. It's very important.

SERGEANT
What's the charge?

OFFICER
Assault with a deadly weapon.

JIM
Listen--

SERGEANT
(annoyed)
He's not here. He's not at
Juvenile Hall. I don't know where he is. He's out on a call and he'll be out all night. How old are you?

JIM
My parents know I'm out. They know
I'm here.

SERGEANT
Come back tomorrow.

JIM
I'll wait for him.

SERGEANT
Why don't you come back tomorrow, son?
(to hoodlum)
Ever been booked before?
JIM turns away, notices a phone on the wall--puts in a coin, asks for a number.
Bedroom of JUDY's parents. Through an open door we hear a radio playing-- a late disc-jockey show for teenagers in which numbers are dedicated by request. JUDY'S MOTHER and
FATHER are in bed, FATHER has phone in his hand.

JUDY'S FATHER
Who wants her? Who? Jim who?
Never heard of you.
He hangs up phone, looks at his wife. She rolls over in bed.

The FATHER turns off the bed lamp, then sits up, worried in the dark.
JUDY's bedroom. It is her radio we have heard. She turns off light, opens the door a crack, and looks out toward her parent's room.

DISSOLVE TO:
Traveling shot. PLATO. He is coming up the walk to his house. When PLATO has come a few feet, somebody whistles.
PLATO and camera stop. Short, quiet whistles come from the boxwood and shrubbery on both sides of the walk. PLATO turns and starts to run, camera following. He gets to his door, tries the key, but in his panic it will not go into the lock. Suddenly a hand reaches in and jerks him around.
CRUNCH stands above him. GOON closes in from the other side.
All very tense and hotted up!

PLATO
What do you want!

CRUNCH
You know what we want. We want your friend.

GOON
We got eyes for him.

PLATO
Listen, you guys ought to go home.
The cops are cruising every--

GOON
Where does he live?
PLATO reaches up swiftly and rings the bell. GOON grabs him.
CRUNCH cracks him.

CRUNCH
You better tell us and I'm not kidding.

PLATO
My old man's got a gun.

GOON
His old man's got a gun. What do you think of that!
(drives a hard blow at PLATO's belly)
Your friend talked--
(belts him again)
Now you talk! Talk!
The door opens and the NEGRO WOMAN is there. CRUNCH sends PLATO spinning into the house past her. He falls.

NEGRO WOMAN
(yelling)
What you doing! What you doing to him! You clear out of here 'fore I call the police!
She swings at CRUNCH who faces her, challenging.

NEGRO WOMAN
Clear out. Go on! Go on now!

MOOSE
Let's go, Crunch.
They turn and move past camera. PLATO gets up off the floor.
We hear the sound of a heap starting. The NEGRO WOMAN closes the door.
Inside PLATO's foyer as NEGRO WOMAN bolts the door.

NEGRO WOMAN
Why you like to mix with bad boys like that? Why you get in trouble all the--

PLATO
I have to go out. I have to warn him.
He starts up the stairs. She follows him heavily.

NEGRO WOMAN
You not going anywhere! You staying home while your mama's away.
Bedroom of PLATO's mother, a lacy affair with imported dolls on the pillows. PLATO
rushes in, opens the drawer of the night-table and pulls out a gun. He checks to see that
it is loaded. The NEGRO WOMAN appears in the door and stares at him, turns on the
light which illuminates the bed-lamp.

NEGRO WOMAN
John! What you doing with that!
You leave that be! Put it down before you hurt yourself. Hear me?
But PLATO moves past her and out of the room. She turns after him.

NEGRO WOMAN
(continuing)
John! You stay home! John! John!
The slam of a door is heard below.

DISSOLVE TO:
JIM's garage. Night. JUDY waiting inside. JIM's car pulls in, a radio going softly. He
turns the motor off and is about to turn off the radio when we hear the announcer:

ANNOUNCER
Coming up now another request--this time from the boys down at Anna's

Pizza Paradise--A new arrangement of a great oldie in rhythm and blues. Jim, this is dedicated to you--from Buzz.
JIM stares at the radio, then turns it off.
Another angle.

JUDY
They'll be looking for you.

JIM
They saw where I jumped! I didn't chicken! What do I have to do-- kill myself?

JUDY
It doesn't matter to them.

JIM
You were looking for me, weren't you?

JUDY
(a small voice)
No--I was just--maybe--

JIM
I tried to call you before.

JUDY
I thought so.

JIM
Want some milk?
JUDY comes forward.

JIM
That's all I can do when I'm nervous. Drink milk. Here--have a slug.
She shakes her head. He takes a sip.

JIM
You still pretty upset?

JUDY
I'm numb.
She is shuddering a little.

JIM
You cold?

JUDY

Even if I'm near a fire, I'm cold.
I guess just about everybody's cold.

JIM
I swear, sometimes, you just want to hold onto somebody! Judy, what am I going to do?
I can't go home again.

JUDY
Neither can I.

JIM
No? Why not?
(no answer)
You know something? Sometimes I figure I'll never live to see my next birthday. Isn't
that dumb?

JUDY
No.

JIM
Every day I look in the mirror and say, "What? You still here?" Man!
They laugh a little.

JIM
Hey! You smiled!
JUDY shakes her head--beginning to warm to him.

JIM
Like even today. I woke up this morning, you know? And the sun was shining and
everything was nice.
Then the first thing that happens is I see you and I thought this is going to be one terrific
day so you better live it up, boy, 'cause tomorrow maybe you'll be nothing.

JUDY
I'm sorry I treated you mean today.
You shouldn't believe what I say when I'm with the kids. Nobody acts sincere.

JIM
Why'd you get mixed up with them?
You don't have to prove anything.

JUDY
If you knew me you wouldn't say that.

JIM
I don't think you trust anybody, do you?

JUDY
Why?

JIM
I'm getting that way, too.

JUDY
(looks at him)
Have you ever gone with anyone who--

JIM
Sure. Lots of times.

JUDY
So have I. But I've never been in love. Isn't that awful?

JIM
(smiling)
Awful? No. It's just lonely.
It's the loneliest time.
She looks up. He kisses her forehead.

JUDY
Why did you do that?

JIM
I felt like it.

JUDY
Your lips are soft when you kiss.
JUDY rises.

JIM
Where you going?

JUDY
I don't know, but we can't stay here.

JIM
Where can we go? I can't go back into that zoo.

JUDY
I'm never going back.

JIM

Listen! I know a place! PLATO showed me before. An old deserted mansion near the planetarium
(rises)
Would you go with me?
JUDY hesitates.

JIM
You can trust me, Judy.

JUDY
I feel as if I'm walking under water.
They start out.

DISSOLVE TO:
Inside bathroom. JIM's house. The water is running in the sink and JIM's father is fixing a stomach settler. Gradually he grows aware of a heavy pounding which insinuates itself above the splash of water. The FATHER pauses, then turns off the tap. The pounding continues. JIM'S MOTHER appears at the bathroom door. She is seen in the mirror tying her robe.

MOTHER
Frank? I'm frightened.

FATHER
What's that pounding?

MOTHER
I don't know. First I thought it was Jim but--

FATHER
He's home. I heard the car.

MOTHER
Are you going down there?

FATHER
Look--just relax, will you?
The pounding ceases.

FATHER
See? It stopped.

MOTHER
I still think you should go down.
He goes out of the bathroom, into the hall.

Foyer. JIM's house as the FATHER comes down the stairs, turning on the light as he comes. He reaches the door and pauses. The MOTHER stops midway down the stairs.

FATHER
(through the door)
Who's there?
(silence)
Anyone there?

MOTHER
(low; at balustrade)
Open it.
The FATHER opens the door and looks up sharply.
Close shot. Door. FATHER's head in f.g. as he stares at it.
Nailed to the door by its outstretched wings, its head hanging in an attitude of crucifixion, is the freshly killed carcass of a chicken. Low whistles are heard from outside.
The FATHER, frightened, looks out into the night.
Full shot. Front lawn and street. Shooting over the
FATHER's head. The whistling continues.

FATHER
(hoarsely)
Who's out there?

VOICE
Where's your son?

FATHER
What?

ANOTHER VOICE
Where's your baby boy gone to,
Daddy? We want him.
Suddenly the FATHER slams the door and rushes past us into the house.
Full shot. Foyer as the FATHER rushes to the bottom of the stairs.

FATHER
Look in his room!
The MOTHER disappears.

FATHER
Jim! Jim!
The FATHER dashes into the living room, then into the hall again and down through the kitchen door.

Back yard as the FATHER comes out. He closes the door quietly and calls in a low voice:

FATHER
Son?
He stares around the yard, then hurries to the garage.
JIM's car is missing. He looks up suddenly.
Reverse shot. JUDY'S FATHER seen across the alley wall. He is standing in his own back yard.

JUDY'S FATHER
Is anything wrong? I'm your neighbor.
Med. shot. JIM'S FATHER. He smiles feebly.

FATHER
Oh, no, thanks. I just wanted to-- to be sure my garage was closed.
JIM'S FATHER closes his garage door and walks back toward his house.

MOTHER (O.S.)
Is he there?

FATHER
No, honey. No, he's not here.
He starts for the house again after a quick look in the direction of JUDY'S FATHER.
Full shot. JUDY's back yard. JUDY'S FATHER watches MR.
STARK disappear, then...

JUDY'S FATHER
(softly)
Judy?
The alley by JIM's house. PLATO drives up on scooter. He checks the garage, sees JIM's car is gone, is about to take off in confusion, hears door slam in JIM's back yard, shuts off engine, fixes tie, combs hair, goes in the fence gate to
JIM's back yard.
Full shot. JIM's back yard. JIM'S FATHER is coming toward him. JIM'S FATHER and PLATO simultaneously say:

FATHER
What are you doing?

PLATO
Where's Jim?

FATHER
I don't know. Do you--do you know where he is?

PLATO

No. No, I don't.

Closeup. PLATO remembers about the mansion--then almost to himself:

PLATO

I know where--

Back to full shot. FATHER and PLATO.

PLATO

Hope I didn't bother you. Goodnight.

He runs to scooter.

FATHER

Hey, come back here. Who are you?

DISSOLVE TO:

Split screen montage. It begins with a telephone ringing alone in the corner of the screen. As camera moves back we see that the phone is in an office at Juvenile Hall. RAY is standing by, trying to make sense out of the incoming reports.

The other part of the screen lights up and becomes:

Bedroom of PLATO'S MOTHER where the NEGRO WOMAN is speaking hysterically into the phone.

Bedroom of JUDY's parents. The FATHER is on the phone.

BEAU has awakened and is crying. His MOTHER tries to divert him.

JIM's bedroom. JIM'S FATHER sits disconsolately on the bed, the phone in his hand. He is talking earnestly.

During this the sound of the telephone ringing has increased to become the sound of many and this has been submerged in a deep rising riot of sirens whose wail mounts higher and higher until:

DISSOLVE TO:

Full shot. Planetarium. Moonlight. A lone siren wails in distance. Aside from this, all is very still. Camera pans past the dome and settles on an isolated mansion set high on a hill nearby. Stone balustrades drop down to sunken gardens where the grass has gone to seed around a waterless fountain.

Closer shot. Mansion. Night. A Mediterranean villa with a large domed solarium which is connected to the main building by a low enclosed arcade. A crash and the falling of splintered glass is heard.

Long shot. Promenade. Shooting through pillars of the main entrance portico, down the long promenade outside arcade.

Two figures, seen in the distance, are disappearing through a window. Camera tracks down promenade until it reaches a broken window through which JIM is just disappearing. When he gets inside, he reaches back and takes his leather jacket which has been spread on the sill to protect them from splinters, shakes it out and puts it on. Running footsteps are heard approaching. JIM looks out nervously. PLATO bursts in, out of breath.

PLATO
Jim!

JIM
Who's that!

PLATO
It's me!

JIM
How'd you find me? What's happening?

PLATO
They're looking for you!--

JIM
Yeah?

PLATO
Everybody! Crunch and Goon and everybody! I think they're going to kill you.

JIM
We know.

PLATO
They think you told the police on them. They--who's in there?

JIM
Judy.

PLATO
Help me in!
JIM gives PLATO a hand over the windowsill.
Inside arcade. JIM and JUDY are seen in an entering shaft of moonlight. PLATO hits
the floor and disappears into darkness.

JIM
Hey where'd you go?

PLATO
I'm here. Shut up.

JIM
Come out come out wherever you are!

PLATO
Shut up. Are you nuts?

JIM
No. I'm scared.
A match flares and lights a candle on an antique Spanish candelabra. PLATO is revealed bending over it. He lights the other candles through the following:

PLATO
We're safe here. I hope.
(holds up candelabra)
What do you think?

JIM
(gazing around)
Wow! Well now-there-then!
His wonderment is justified. The floor of the arcade is marble and there are marble benches and neo-Roman busts lining the walls.

PLATO
Isn't it crazy?

JIM
Wowee ow wow! Let's take it for the summer.

JUDY
Oh, Jim!

JIM
No--come on. Should we rent or are we in a buying mood, dear?

JUDY
(laughing)
You decide, darling. Remember our budget.

PLATO
Don't give it a thought. Only three million dollars a month!

JUDY
Oh, we can manage that! I'll scrimp and save and work my fingers to the bone...

JIM
Why don't we just rent it for the season?

JUDY
You see, we've just--oh, you tell him, darling. I'm so embarrassed I could die!

JIM
Well--we're newlyweds.

JUDY
There's just one thing. What about--

PLATO
Children? Well, we really don't encourage them. They're so noisy and troublesome, don't you agree?

JUDY
Yes. And so terribly annoying when they cry. I just don't know what to do when they cry, do you dear?

JIM
Of course. Drown them like puppies.

JUDY
See, we're very modern.

PLATO
Shall I show you the nursery? It's far away from the rest of the house.
If you have children--Oh I hate the word!--or if you decide to adopt one--they can carry on and you'll never even notice. In fact, if you lock them in you never have to see them again, much less talk to them.

JUDY
Talk to them! Heavens!

JIM
Nobody talks to children! They just tell them one thing and mean another.

PLATO
It's wonderful that you understand so well--and so young too! You know the most wonderful feature about the nursery?

JIM
What?

PLATO
There's only one key.

JIM
We'll take it!

PLATO
Come on!
PLATO leads them away from us down the arcade, the candelabra casting wild shadows on the walls. They are laughing as they disappear through the glass doors at the end and their laughter echoes stonily.

DISSOLVE TO:
Med. shot. A street and an alley. Night seen through the windshield of a police car. Its radio is on low. Two officers are in the front seat. One of them drinks coffee from a container. Suddenly MOOSE's heap moves past on the street ahead. In it are MOOSE, GOON and CRUNCH.
Full shot. The street as MOOSE's heap continues up the empty street. The police car slides out of the alley where it has been concealed, and follows at a distance. Its headlights are off.
Close shot. CRUNCH, GOON and MOOSE (Process). They are in the front seat of MOOSE's heap.

MOOSE
What time is it?

CRUNCH
Hang loose. We got all night.

MOOSE
That maid saw us. She could identify us too.

CRUNCH
You still want to go home, Moose?

MOOSE
No.

CRUNCH
Then shut your mouth before your guts run out!

GOON
What guts?

DISSOLVE TO:
Inside glass solarium. A swimming pool lies at the center.
There is no water in it. Framing the pool is a flagstone walk with marble benches spotted here and there. The great glass room had once been planted thickly with tropical foliage. But now what palms and lianas remain are withered and dead with lack of care. At the edge of the pool, near the deep end, a blanket has been spread and a candelabra burns upon it. In its mysterious light our three kids are revealed:
JIM, bouncing precariously at the end of the diving board;

JUDY on the blanket nearby; PLATO on the pool's bottom. All three are laughing hysterically when suddenly JIM starts to lose his balance.

JIM
(yelling)
Quick! Fill the pool!
JIM falls in. PLATO rushes to him.

JIM
Let's see how long we can stay under.

PLATO
Man, you're schizoid!

JIM
(in another outburst of laughing)
I'm what? What?

JUDY
You can't talk underwater!

JIM
(gargling)
I bet you hear everything I say!

PLATO
(gargling)
Isn't he schizoid?

JIM
(gargling)
Hey! How 'bout that!
They laugh again. JIM swings up the ladder and goes to JUDY.
PLATO follows.

PLATO
Haven't you noticed your personality splitting?

JIM
Not lately.
They all sit on the blanket.

JIM
How do you know so much about this junk, Plato?

PLATO

I had to go to a head-shrinker. I only went twice though. My mother said it cost too much, so she went to Hawaii instead.
JIM lies back with his head in JUDY's lap. She strokes his hair and smiles at him. PLATO looks away.

JIM
No. Seriously. What's your trouble?
PLATO hesitates a moment, then leans back, cuddling between the two of them.

PLATO
I don't know but whatever it is, it's gone now. I mean I'm happy now. Here.
JIM puts his arm under PLATO's chin.

PLATO
I came here before.

JIM
When was that?

PLATO
When I was here? When I ran away.
I used to run away a lot but they always took me back.

JIM
Who?

PLATO
Mom and Dad. I used to be in my crib and I'd listen to them fight.

JIM
You remember that far back? Boy, I can't even remember yesterday.

JUDY
Plato, where's your father now?

PLATO
He's dead. He was a hero in the
China Sea.

JIM
You told me he's a big wheel in New
York!

PLATO
I did? Well, he might as well be dead. What's the difference?

JUDY
It's all right.

JIM
Sure.
PLATO closes his eyes. JUDY hums a lullaby as she strokes
JIM's lips with a finger. He snaps at it. Then he kisses her hand, looks at her palm. They
whisper.

JIM
(continuing)
You have a long life-line.
She takes his palm and examines it.

JUDY
So have you.
She kisses it, holds her cheek against it.

JIM
Ever been in a place like this before?

JUDY
Not exactly. It's certainly huge.

JIM
How many rooms do you think there are?

JUDY
I don't know.

JIM
Should we explore?
She looks at PLATO. JIM shrugs--tests to see if the boy is awake, but there is no
reaction.
Carefully, they crawl to their feet. JIM supporting PLATO's head with his hands as they
do so. JIM takes the other blanket and covers PLATO with it. JUDY kneels on the other
side and tucks it in. They look at each other across him and smile. Then suddenly JUDY
bends down and kisses PLATO's cheek very softly. JUDY and JIM rise.
JIM takes a candle from the candelabra and leads JUDY along the edge of the pool to
the glass doors beyond. Silence except for their footfalls on the flagstone. In the distance
we see the doors open and the couple pass through.
When they close again, a sob comes from PLATO.
High angle closeup. PLATO lying as they left him, but his eyes are open and he is
crying. Camera booms up as PLATO throws off the blanket and looks after them.
Camera booms higher until he is revealed as a small and lonely figure sitting by himself.
The pool echoes his weeping.

DISSOLVE TO:
Inside library. Mansion. Night. The door opens slowly and
JIM appears with the candle. JUDY lingers at the door. The flickering light reveals a
formerly lavish room, paneled in oak. There is a tapestry couch, empty bookcases, some
dim portraits, a leather table and several chairs around a great stone fireplace.

JIM
Hey! Will you look at this room!
(looks behind him)
Judy?
She comes forward. JIM drips wax on the table-top and sticks the candle on it. His hand
shakes. JUDY sits on the couch.

JIM
(continuing)
Want to read any books? Take your pick!
(sits beside her)
Isn't this the craziest?

JUDY
Hi.

JIM
Hi.
He takes her hand. She looks at him and smiles.

JIM
(continuing)
What?

JUDY
Your hand's all wet and it's shaky.
(kisses it)
You're so funny.

JIM
Why?

JUDY
I don't know--you just are.
Leaving a light for Plato. That was nice.

JIM
Maybe he's scared of the dark.

JUDY
Are you?
JIM snuffs out the candle. They are left in moonlight. A pause.

JIM
(singing)
Here we are-- out of cigarettes--
Junior's in the nurs'ry--
See how late it gets--

JUDY
You don't need to do that.

JIM
There's something I should tell you, Judy.

JUDY
I know already. We don't have to pretend now.

JIM
(laughing)
What a relief!
He leans back, relaxed at last. She snuggles close to him.

JUDY
Is this what it's like to love somebody?

JIM
You disappointed?

JUDY
(mussing her hair)
Funny Jimmy. You're so clean and you--this is silly.

JIM
What?

JUDY
You smell like baby powder.

JIM
So do you.

JUDY
I never felt so clean before.

JIM
It's not going to be lonely, Judy.
Not for you and not for me.

JUDY
I love somebody. All the time I've been looking for someone to love me and now--I
love somebody. And it's so easy. Why is it easy now?

JIM
It is for me too.

JUDY
I love you, Jim. I really mean it.
She kisses his lips gently and looks into his face. He returns the kiss. Their arms go
around each other.

JIM
I mean it too.
He kisses her again--
Full shot. Road near Planetarium. MOOSE's heap crawls up and turns left. A moment
later, the police car appears and does likewise--still holding its distance.
Full shot. The mansion as MOOSE's heap moves past on the road below. Suddenly it
stops.
Inside MOOSE's heap. CRUNCH looks off, curious.

GOON
What you stopping for?

CRUNCH
You scam a car up there?

MOTHER
So what?

CRUNCH
Nobody's lived in that hunk of junk for five-six years.
He switches on the spotlight. It illuminates JIM's heap.

CRUNCH
Well, what do you know! I feel a kick coming on!
He turns off all the lights and gets out. The others follow.
Med. shot. Police car. It has halted. One of the officers gets out and draws his gun. The
other makes radio contact in a low voice:

OFFICER
This is Unit 17. Unit 17.

RADIO
Come in, Unit 17.

OFFICER
We just zeroed three kids in a heap.
Crest Drive and Observatory. Looks like house-breaking. Send us some help. They may
be armed. Over.
Close shot. PLATO asleep on the blanket. Only a single candle burns in the candelabra.
The same low whistles heard earlier come from all around him and rise in volume.
Suddenly his eyes open. He doesn't move, but he has come suddenly awake.
Low shot. PLATO lying in f.g. Next to his face are a pair of booted feet. He looks up.
Camera pans up to show CRUNCH.
He is smiling. He holds a tire chain in his hand which he swings.

CRUNCH
Good morning.
Full shot. The swimming pool. GOON and MOOSE are behind
CRUNCH. They too are armed with tire chains. They all laugh. PLATO rolls away from
them and runs toward the deep end of the pool.

CRUNCH
Moose! Take the steps! Goon! The other side.
The boys run to their assigned places. PLATO sees no exit.
He flings himself down the ladder and into the pool. He feints this way and that, the
boys responding as if they were fencing. CRUNCH swings down the ladder and his
boots make a loud report as they hit the pool. MOOSE advances down the steps at the
shallow end. GOON climbs onto the pool bottom at the opposite side. The feinting
continues, wordlessly, as the circle closes around PLATO. The only sounds are the
stamping of their boots as they try to distract him from side to side, and the animalistic
grunts they make to scare him. Suddenly PLATO sees an opening and plunges past
MOOSE, pushing him over, and stumbles up the steps.

CRUNCH
Come on! Let's make it!
They stream out of the pool after PLATO. He reaches the glass doors first, streaks
though, and bangs them shut behind him.
Traveling shot. Arcade. PLATO's face is visible only when the moonlight strikes him
through the passing windows. The sound of running steps behind him.
Full shot. Main room. A pattern of moonlight on the bare floor as PLATO dashes in and
through it. He falls over a piece of furniture and comes scurrying in to camera, wheels
around on hands and knees to face the door. The boys plunge into the moonlit square
and stop. PLATO tries not to breathe. A match is struck. CRUNCH looks around, but
can see nothing. That match goes out. The boys start up the stairs, whispering.
Immediately, PLATO crawls forward, under the piano. He hears a murmur of voices
from behind the oak door of the library--next to the piano. He moves to it stealthily.

Close shot, PLATO at door listening through it, on hands and knees. His confusion mounts. He shakes his head to clear it. Then, suddenly he rises and tries the knob. The door is locked. He beats on it.

PLATO
Save me!
The boys run across the room. As they hit the moonlit square. PLATO spins and fires. Somebody drops and starts moaning. JIM opens the door.

PLATO
(shrieks)
What you run out on me for! What you leave me alone for?

JIM
Plato!
There is a rush of boys coming forward.

PLATO
(with hate)
I don't want you for my father!

JIM
Your father!
PLATO fires at JIM. JIM leaps at PLATO with a cry and knocks him down.

JIM
(in rage)
You crazy nut! You crazy, crazy nut!

PLATO
(screaming)
Get away from me!
He rolls away from JIM and runs to the main door.

JUDY
Jim!
Main door, from inside. PLATO falls upon it, fumbles with the bolt and swings the door wide. He steps out into the waning moonlight and we see him running down the lawn. JIM rushes into the doorway and stops short.
Full shot. Mansion. The OFFICERS are moving away from us toward it. PLATO runs wildly toward them.

OFFICER
(sharply)
Halt!
PLATO stops, confused.

OFFICER
(continuing)
Come here.
JIM runs out on the promenade and starts over the balustrade.

JIM
Plato!
Close shot. PLATO. His face is working desperately in growing panic.

OFFICER (O.S.)
Come here, son.

PLATO
No!

JIM (O.S.)
Plato!

OFFICER (O.S.)
Just walk over here quietly now-- and there won't be any trouble.
PLATO runs out.
Close shot. JIM as he screams.

JIM
Plato!
Full shot. Main doorway as JUDY rushes out, followed by
GOON and MOOSE. They all stop dead at the balustrade.

JUDY
Jim! Watch out!
Reverse shot. Lawn. JIM seen in f.g. PLATO bolting toward the woods in the direction
of the planetarium. The officers have both hit the ground in the distance. They fire again.
JIM hesitates a moment, then rushes after PLATO. The officers fire again.
Moving shot. JIM as he runs after PLATO.
Med. shot. OFFICERS as they rise to their feet.

FIRST OFFICER
Take the house! I'll head him off.
Full shot. Front of mansion. JUDY flies down the stairs and rushes past camera.

OFFICER (O.S.)
Halt! Halt!
Prowl car. Another part of town (Process). RAY is driving.
JIM's father is beside him. The mother is in the back seat.

RADIO

--located at Summit Drive--the
Planetarium.

RAY
(snapping on mike)
The planetarium? One kid inside-- five housebreaking in area. Will proceed.
(turning to JIM's parents)
There are some kids in trouble-- you'll have to go with me.

FATHER
Perfectly all right.
Edge of woods as JIM hurtles in from the open ground beyond.
He stumbles against a tree and sinks down.

JIM
(yelling)
Plato!
Traveling shot in the woods as PLATO rushes through the moonlit trees, sobbing.

JIM (O.S.)
(distant)
Plato!
Med. shot. JIM at the base of a tree. He is whimpering, shaking his head. JUDY crashes
through the brush and drops beside him.

JUDY
Did he hit you?
She is on the verge of hysteria.

JIM
No!

JUDY
We have to go back!

JIM
No! I got to find him.
He starts to rise.

JUDY
After he tried to shoot you?

JIM
He didn't mean it--we shouldn't have left him. He needed us.

JUDY

He needed you, maybe. So do I.
There is a sound of distant gunfire. Both kids freeze.

JIM
He needs you too. Come on.
JUDY, breaking into a run, follows after him through the brush.

JUDY
You should have heard him talk about you tonight. Like you were the hero in the China Seas.

JIM
Sure. He was trying to make us his family.

JUDY
They're killing him!
JIM runs ahead blindly and disappears in the trees. JUDY rushes after him a few steps, then stops.
JUDY and JIM running.
PLATO running.
The planetarium. Moonlight. Shooting from the bridle path and panning to the building.
PLATO reels in and goes to the front door.
Med. shot. Door to planetarium. PLATO clutches the handle.
The door is locked. He whimpers once in frustration.
Med. shot. Policeman running up same path PLATO has followed.
PLATO at door to planetarium. He smashes the glass with his gun and dives through.
Inside planetarium as PLATO lands. He is cut and bleeding.

OFFICER (O.S.)
Come out of there.
PLATO wheels and skitters backward across the floor of the observatory on his hands and knees until he comes to the door of the planetarium theater.
Reverse shot. Main entrance. Seen from inside. The
OFFICER in b.g., PLATO in f.g. The OFFICER appears in the entrance, then moves quickly to one side to be less of a target. He reaches in to unlatch the door.

OFFICER
You're making it tough on yourself, kid. Come out quietly now. You didn't kill anybody yet.
PLATO fires at him, then opens the door of the planetarium theater and runs inside. The door swings shut behind him.
Outside planetarium. The OFFICER is hugging the outside wall. Another siren wails and a spotlight catches the
OFFICER who runs out into the light.

OFFICER

(running)
Need a little help here!
Full shot. Parking lot as the CHIEF's car wheels to a stop.
It is followed by a civilian car and a cab.
CHIEF's car.

CHIEF
We heard firing. He get anybody?
You alone?

OFFICER
We got a cookaboo inside. He wounded some kid earlier.

CHIEF
How'd he get in?

OFFICER
Smashed the front door.

CHIEF
Any other entrance?

OFFICER
(leaving)
Down in back.
Med. shot. Bushes bordering planetarium as JIM climbs through them and stops short,
staring in amazement. JUDY is in b.g.
Full shot. Parking lot. JIM seen in f.g. hiding in the screen of leaves. Beyond we see the
full activity--the crowd, the cars, searchlights playing on the planetarium entrance,
police moving in under direction of the CHIEF.

CHIEF
(loud on speaker)
Silence. Please maintain silence.
Keep back and stay off the pavements. Keep back and stay off the pavements. There
will be emergency vehicles coming through.
This warning is for your own protection.
RAY's prowl car come in. JIM's parents climb out, curious.
RAY hurries to consult with an officer who briefs him, then hurries to the chief's car.
Parking lot. Several patrol cars now line the parking lot.
The NEGRO WOMAN in her nightgown and overcoat pushes forward from a cab and
accosts an OFFICER.

NEGRO WOMAN
What's going on?

OFFICER

I don't know, lady. Some kid's in trouble. Stand back, please.

NEGRO WOMAN

I got to know. My boy run off tonight. He had a gun with him, too.
Med. shot. CHIEF's car as RAY hurries in.

CHIEF

Hello, Ray--Know anything about this?

RAY

As much as you do--Loan me your mike, will you?

CHIEF

(handing it to him)
Help yourself.

RAY

(into mike)
I am addressing the boy in the planetarium. I am speaking to the boy inside. This is Ray
Framek from the Juvenile Division--
Close-up JIM as he reacts to RAY's name. He rises and looks off.

RAY (O.S.)

(over speaker)
You are now surrounded. You are surrounded by many armed police.
Whoever you are, drop your weapon and come outside.
Med. shot. JIM'S FATHER standing by RAY's car, gazing off with interest. His wife
comes out and stands beside him, looks at him questioningly.

RAY (O.S.)

(over speaker)
Come outside. Clasp your hands over your head and come outside quietly--
The FATHER's gaze has traveled over the scene. Suddenly he sees his son followed by
JUDY, run into the planetarium.

MOTHER

Frank!

FATHER

Stay here.
(goes over to RAY)
That was my son!

RAY

You sure?

FATHER
I think I know my son.
The FATHER moves behind the crowd, camera trucking with him, until he reaches the bushes at the edge of the parking lot and stops, gathering himself. Meanwhile RAY's voice continues over:

RAY (O.S.)
(over speaker)
Jim Stark! I'm addressing Jim
Stark. Nobody will harm you or your friends if you follow these instructions. We are here to protect you. Drop your guns and come outside. Nobody will hurt you if you do as I say--
The FATHER starts forward along the bushes as if stalking game. Each step is carefully placed and quiet, but his heart tugs him along like a kite dragging an anchor.

CHIEF
Officers! Another boy and girl just ran into the planetarium. We do not know if they are armed.
Hold your positions until further instruction.
Inside planetarium as JIM comes dashing in, spins around, staring. JUDY follows. A siren is heard outside growing shrill.

CHIEF (O.S.)
(over speaker)
Ambulance. Ambulance is coming through. Clear a passage. Will you people make way there?
Floodlights strike the door and illuminate the lobby dimly.

JIM
(softly)
Plato?
Silence. JIM moves cautiously to the door of the planetarium theater. JUDY hangs back. Another siren is heard approaching. More floodlights strike the door.

JIM
(continuing - calling softly)
Plato? Plato, you in there?
(silence)
Hey, I'm going to open the door now.
You'll be able to see me and you can shoot me if you want, but just remember one thing, Plato--You're my friend. That means a lot to me.
JIM opens the door slowly.
Inside theater. Darkness except for the splash of light from the door where JIM stands in silhouette. He lets the door close. Blackness.

JIM
Plato?

PLATO
I'm here.

JIM
Boy, I'm blind as a bat! You got a match? I'm going to break my neck in here. Where
are you?

PLATO
I've got a gun.

JIM
I know. Light a match, will you?
PLATO obeys.

JIM
That's swell. How are you?

PLATO
I'm fine.
Another siren is heard outside. JIM has reached the lecturer's desk and, just as the match
goes out, he throws a switch. The stars appear on the dome and the projector starts its
slow revolution.

PLATO
You think the end of the world will come at nighttime, Jim?

JIM
No. At dawn.

PLATO
Why?

JIM
I just have a feeling. Where are you?

PLATO
Here.

JIM
Well, stop hiding and stand up. I can't talk to you if I don't see you.
JIM waits. Nothing happens.

JIM

Hey, look at the stars, Plato.
Stand up and look at the stars.
Plato rises from behind a row, then JIM continues:

JIM
That's fine.
JIM approaches slowly.

JIM
I'm not going to hurt you.

PLATO
Why did you run out on me?

JIM
We didn't run out. We were coming right back.

PLATO
You sure?

JIM
Sure I'm sure. Judy's waiting.
You ready to come out now?
A siren is heard.

PLATO
No.

JIM
I promise nothing'll happen if you do.
(silence)
You want my jacket? It's warm.
JIM takes off his jacket and holds it out to PLATO.

PLATO
Can I keep it?

JIM
What do you think?
JIM gives him the jacket--PLATO puts it on.

JIM
You want to give me your gun now,
Plato?

PLATO

My gun?

JIM
In your pocket. Give it to me.

PLATO
I need it.

JIM
You trust me, don't you? Just give it to me for a second.
PLATO hands him the gun. JIM removes the cartridges and puts them in his pocket.

PLATO
You promised to give it back.

JIM
Friends never break promises, do they?
(gives him back the gun)
Okay. Here. Now listen. There are a lot of people outside and they all want you to be safe. You understand that? They said I could come in and bring you out.

PLATO
Why?

JIM
They like you. Okay?

PLATO
Come on!
JIM opens the door for PLATO, then follows him out. JUDY joins them.

JUDY
Hi, Plato!

PLATO
Hi.
Observatory as JIM, JUDY and PLATO come to the entrance.
PLATO sees an OFFICER.

PLATO
Who's that?

JIM
Just a guard.

PLATO

I shot at one of them.

JIM
But you didn't hurt anybody.
Outside observatory as PLATO and JIM come forward into the early dawn. PLATO stops and looks off, scared.
Slow pan shot. The crowd. It has grown enormously.
Silence. There are armed officers everywhere--all waiting, alert.
Med. shot. NEGRO WOMAN. Her eyes are moist. Her lips move in silent prayer.
Med. shot. JIM's parents. The FATHER looking on anxiously.
The MOTHER is crying against the car.
Med. shot. JIM and PLATO.

PLATO
Those aren't my friends. Make them go away.

JIM
(tense; calling past camera)
Ray! Will you tell these guys to move back?
Suddenly PLATO bolts. JIM wheels after him.

JIM
(yelling)
Plato! Don't be a fool!
Full shot. Planetarium as PLATO dashes to the stairway leading to the balcony.
JIM'S FATHER and MOTHER. Their faces reflect panic as they see PLATO running in JIM's coat.

MOTHER
It's Jim!
Full shot. Balcony. Shooting down the stairs as PLATO rushes up. JIM closes behind him. Camera pans with PLATO as he climbs the ladder to the ledge of the small dome. JIM stops at the foot of the ladder.

JIM
Plato!

PLATO
Keep away from me! I don't believe you anymore!
He raises the gun as if to shoot JIM. An OFFICER drops to one knee and fires a shot at PLATO.
Full shot. Small dome. PLATO drops like a stone to JIM's feet.
Close-up. JIM.

JIM
(screaming--wildly)

But I've got the bullets! The gun was empty!
Close shot. NEGRO WOMAN as she screams, a handkerchief in her mouth.
Close shot. JUDY. She sobs once and runs up steps.
Med. shot. JIM staring down at PLATO.

JIM
Plato?
(crouches over PLATO)
Plato. Hey, Jerkpot!
There is nothing. He rises and faces the crowd, shaking his head in wonder and reproach.

JIM
(quiet)
What did you have to do that for?
Full shot, the roof. Parents and Officers. The NEGRO WOMAN is hysterical. RAY
shoves past her, followed by JIM'S
FATHER and MOTHER. They rush toward camera.
Ambulance crew. They spring into action, arrive with stretcher.
The balcony. JIM is at PLATO's side. A couple of OFFICERS rush forward to take JIM.
The FATHER comes in and pushes them aside.

FATHER
Let him alone! He's mine! I'll take care of him!
RAY, who has witnessed this, motions to the officers.

RAY
It's all right! It's all right!
The FATHER stares down at JIM for a moment. Then he kneels beside his son, puts his
coat over JIM's shoulders. He speaks very gently.

FATHER
For a minute...that jacket...I thought...
(breaks off, then)
You couldn't help it, son.
(reaches out, gently, but firmly)
You did everything a man could do.
He takes JIM by the elbow and starts to bring him to his feet. The boy suddenly resists,
and remains kneeling.

FATHER
Stand up, Jim. I'll stand up with you. Let me try to be as strong as you want me to be.
A faint hope appears in the boy's face. He no longer resists as the FATHER helps him
to rise. But he still keeps his back to him. The ambulance attendants start putting
PLATO on a stretcher. JIM moves, as if to stop them, but the FATHER still holds his
shoulders.
JIM

He depended on me.

FATHER
And you can depend on me, son.
Trust me. Whatever comes we'll face it together, I swear.
JIM feels, for the first time, the love and security he has always wanted. He clutches at his FATHER, crying unashamedly.
The FATHER's arms envelop him. PLATO, through his death, has helped these two find each other.
Close shot. JUDY and RAY watching.
Low angle. NEGRO WOMAN as she bends over PLATO's body.

NEGRO WOMAN
(as they lift PLATO onto litter)
This poor baby got nobody. Just nobody.
As he is carried past her, she follows.
Balcony stairs. From below as JIM, supported by his FATHER, comes down. RAY is behind them. They pause for a silent meeting with the MOTHER at foot of the stairs. She kisses
JIM and starts wiping his tears away, but he is weeping soundlessly and it does no good.
JIM looks back up at the dome. The ambulance attendants are bearing PLATO's litter down the last few stairs, followed by the NEGRO WOMAN.
Group. The ambulance attendants come down the last few stairs followed by the NEGRO WOMAN. JIM steps forward suddenly and adjusts the blanket covering PLATO. JUDY comes to JIM's side. The litter passes camera and we hold on two shot of JIM and JUDY, seen against the lightening sky.

JIM
(to JUDY, half to himself)
He was always cold.
JUDY moves to JIM and touches his arm lightly. He looks down at her.
Med. shot. The group. JIM's arm is around JUDY as he leads her, firmly, towards his MOTHER and FATHER. His voice is warm, brimming with the new found pride he takes in his parents as he introduces JUDY to them.

JIM
Mom--Dad--this is my friend. Her name is Judy.
The parents nods warmly and smile at her. She smiles shyly in response, happy at being accepted. There is a warmth emanating from the tight little group. Changes have happened to them. Old things have been shed and a new start has been made. Camera booms--pulls back high to:
High general shot. Planetarium, JIM and JUDY, FATHER and
MOTHER threading their way through the crowd as the camera continues to pull back.

FADE OUT.

The end.